ON THE STREET OF DIVINE LOVE

PITT POETRY SERIES

Ed Ochester, Editor

ON THE STREET OF DIVINE LOVE

NEW AND SELECTED POEMS

BARBARA HAMBY

UNIVERSITY OF PITTSBURGH PRESS

Published by the University of Pittsburgh Press, Pittsburgh, Pa., 15260
Copyright © 2014, Barbara Hamby
Manufactured in the United States of America
Printed on acid-free paper
10 9 8 7 6 5 4 3 2 1

ISBN 13: 978-0-8229-6288-5
ISBN 10: 0-8229-6288-8

for
my sister
Quincie Hamby

My God! Where is everyone? I can't sleep on this bed of gold. Give it all away. Light comes only from divine love. The world is a theater of everything we want. Goodbye monsters, hallucinations, catastrophes.

The perfect song of angels rises from the rescue ship. It is divine love. Two loves! I can die of my love for God or my love of the world. I have left those whose wounds will be deeper by my betrayal. Among the lost you choose me, but the others—are they not dear to me?

Save them!

—ARTHUR RIMBAUD, *A SEASON IN HELL*

CONTENTS

Babel (2004)

All-Night Lingo Tango (2009)

ON THE STREET OF DIVINE LOVE

NEW POEMS

Ode to Forgetting the Year

Forget the year, the parties where you drank too much,
        said what you thought without thinking, danced so hard
you dislocated your hip, fainted in the kitchen,
        while Gumbo, your hosts' Jack Russell terrier,
looked you straight in the eye, bloomed into a boddhisattva,
        lectured you on the Six Perfections while drunk people
with melting faces gathered around your shimmering corpse.

Then there was February when you should have been decapitated
        for stupidity. Forget those days and the ones
when you faked a smile so stale it crumbled like a cookie
        down the side of your face. Forget the crumbs and the mask
you wore and the tangle of Scotch tape you used to keep it in place,

but then you'd have to forget spring with its clouds of jasmine,
        wild indigo, and the amaryllis with their pink and red faces,
your garden with its twelve tomato plants, squash, zucchini,
        nine kinds of peppers, okra, and that disappointing row of corn.
Forget the corn, its stunted ears and brown oozing tips. Forgive
        the worms that sucked their flesh like zombies
and forgive the bee that stung your arm, then stung your face, too.

While we're at it, let's forget 1974. You should have died that year,
        or maybe you did. Resurrection's a trick
you learned early. And 2003. You could have called in sick
        those twelve months—sick and silly, illiterate and numb,

and summer, remember the day at the beach when the sun
        began to explain Heidegger to you while thunderclouds
rumbled up from the horizon like Nazi submarines? The fried oysters
        you ate later at Angelo's were a consolation and the margaritas

with salt and ice. Remember how you begged the sullen teenaged waitress
        to bring you a double, and double that, pleasepleaseplease.

And forget all the crime shows you watched,
        the DNA samples, hair picked up with tweezers
and put in plastic bags, the grifters, conmen, and the husbands
        who murdered their wives for money or just plain fun.
Forget them and the third grade and your second boyfriend,
        who loved *Blonde on Blonde* as much as you did
but wanted something you wouldn't be able to give anyone for years.

Forget movies, too, the Hollywood trash in which nothing happened
        though they were loud and fast, and when they were over
time had passed, which was a blessing in itself. O blessed
        is Wong Kar-wai and his cities of blue and rain.
Blessed is David Lynch, his Polish prostitutes juking
        to "The Loco-Motion" in a kitschy fifties bungalow. Blessed
is Leonard Cohen, his "Hallelujah" played a thousand times
        as you drove through Houston, its vacant lots
exploding with wild flowers and capsized shopping carts.

So forget the pizzas you ate, the ones you made from scratch
        and the Domino's ordered in darkest December,
the plonk you washed it down with and your Christmas tree
        with the angel you found in Naples and the handmade Santas
your sons brought home from school, the ones with curling eyelashes
        and vampire fangs. Forget their heartbreaks
and your sleepless nights like gift certificates
        from *The Twilight Zone*, because January's here,
and the stars are singing a song you heard on a street corner once,
        so wild the pavement rippled, and it called you
like the night calls you with his monsters and his marble arms.

How to Pray

Falling down on your knees is the easy part, like drinking
        a glass of cold water on a hot day, the parched straw
of your throat flooded, your knees hitting the ground,
        a prizefighter in the final rounds. You're bloody,
your bones like iron ties, hands trembling in the dust. What
        do you do with your hands? Clasp them together
as if you're keeping your heart between your palms,
        like their namesakes in the desert oasis,
because that's what you're looking for now, a place
        where you can rest. It has been a dry ride for months,
sand filling your mouth, crusting your half-blind eyes,
        and you need to speak to someone—though who
you don't really know. Pardon is on your mind. Perhaps
        you could talk to your mother. You are fifteen
and think her life is over. You don't say it, but you think it,
        and she's ten years younger than you are now,
her hair still dark. How do you thank her for waking up
        each morning and taking on a day that would kill you
and not just one but thousands? How do you thank her
        for the way she tossed words around and made them
spin and laugh and do cartwheels on the lawn?
        And your father, he's the one who loved poetry,
bought the book that opened your world to you
        like someone cutting into a birthday cake the gods
have baked just for her. Do you talk to him about not caring
        and teaching you that same cool touch?
And King James, how do you thank him for all the words
        his scribes took from Wycliff and Tyndall, and Keats
for his odes, and Neruda for his. But this wasn't meant to be a prayer
        of thanksgiving but a scourge with a hair shirt and whips
and bowls of gruel. But is it blood the gods need,

or should your offering be all you have—words
and too many of them to count on the fingers pressed to your lips,
or maybe not enough and never the right ones.

Ode to Knots, Noise, Waking Up at Three, and Falling Asleep Reading to My Id

Why does everything seems so impossible
     in the middle of the night? I wake up at three
with my mind in a knot, and I might as well be Incan,
     the ancient people of Peru, whose language
was not written in characters like the Chinese
     or letters like the Greeks and Romans or even runes
like the Celts, but knots on a string, so maybe when the Incans
     woke up at three, they could feel their knots,
whereas all I can do is review my worries or recite the poems
     I've memorized, a couple of sonnets by Shakespeare
and Donne, Hamlet's "What a piece of work is a man" speech
     and all the lyrics to *Highway 61 Revisited,* my favorite being
"Just Like Tom Thumb's Blues," because when the lights
     are out you might as well be lost in the rain in Juárez,
and sometimes I forget how uncooperative the material world
     can be, though at moments all the pieces fit
like a Byzantine mosaic, which I'm thinking about now
     because I'm going to Ravenna tomorrow,
and I can't sleep because the Piazza Sant'Ambrogio,
     which is right outside my bedroom window,
has become a late night hangout for braying drunks—God,
     the lungs on those people—and I can't help but think
of all my mistakes as they line up like the bloody crucifixions
     I've been seeing in Italy this spring,
though the sky has been a glorious Leonardo blue, and the names
     of the artists, how could you not be great with a name
like Duccio di Buoninsegna, and you'd have to go a long way
     to find a better name than Dosso Dossi, so toss and turn
as I may, it is not Eastertime, but the beginning of June,
     and it was Luis Buñuel who said, *Thank God*

I'm an atheist, though my Bulgarian student Polina
                    says that God is in other people, and it's hard
not to believe in other people since there are so many of them,
                    their screams bouncing off the Renaissance walls
of Sant'Ambrogio and into my window, and my train leaves
                    at 7:30, and what if my mother has a stroke,
and there's no one there to help her, and all my cats line up
                    and list my betrayals: Annabelle, Sylvia Wilberforce,
Little Latin Loopy Lulu, and Bucky, aka Mr. Suit Pants,
                    Mr. Crazy Bacon, Mr. Pretty Paws, and I hope
he's in a paradise where lost tails are sewn back on
                    and torn ears mended, because I've had it up to here
with the everyday scarring, the laundry, the dust, so I might as well
                    be asleep and dreaming of the tomb of Galla Placidia in Ravenna,
the night sky made of thousands of pieces of colored tesserae,
                    or facing a tidal wave in a South American town
or riding a bus when a fat man in tighty-whities and a black
                    T-shirt gets on and starts shooting, blood flying
everywhere, but soon he's bored by the mayhem and sits down
                    beside me and asks what I am doing. Moving to keep
his bloody arm away from my white dress, I say, "Reading
                    a newspaper." "What's that?" he asks. "It's where
you read about what happened the day before." "Read,"
                    he says, so I tell him about all the terrible
things people did yesterday in buses all over the world.

Ode to Skimpy Clothes and August in the Deep South

A young woman is walking with her boyfriend, and it's deep
        summer in the South, like being in a sauna
but hotter and stickier, and she's wearing a tank top
        and a cotton skirt so thin I can see her black
underpants, and this is the way I dressed in my early twenties,
        partly from poverty and partly because my body
was so fresh that I couldn't imagine not showing it off—
        marzipan arms, breasts like pink cones of vanilla
soft-serve ice cream, hips more like brioche than flesh,
        and the sound track to those times I can conjure
on my inner radio on a day in August—"Wild Horses,"
        and "All I Want," Joni Mitchell and Mick Jagger
singing a duet for me, but I was in love with Bartok, too,
        and Beethoven's trios, moving through those sultry days
to that celestial music, going to the campus cinema for the air
        conditioning and *Wild Strawberries* and *La Dolce Vita*,
skin brown from taking the Chevy pickup to the coast,
        at night putting the fan in the window and reading
thick novels until three or four, and one morning waking at noon
        to a cardinal screaming, the red male hovering,
flying above, my cat with the brown female in her mouth,
        and when I release the bird she falls on the grass as if dead,
but she's in shock, and I hold the cat, who wants her again,
        but then the bird comes to, hops across the grass
and flies off with her mate, and seeing that girl's black panties
        under her skirt brings back those days with such a fierce ache
that I might as well be lost in the outskirts of Rome, a little girl
        making up a story of seeing the Virgin and everyone
wanting to believe that God has appeared in the parking lot
        of an abandoned store, the graffiti a message, something
divine in the plastic bags and fast-food boxes rolling in the wind.

Ode to Lil' Kim in Florence

We're in a taxi on the way to see Andrea del Sarto's Last Supper,
      which was in the country when it was painted
but now in the suburbs beyond the old city wall in an ex-convent,
      and our driver turns the radio to an English station
playing an American song, yes, Lil' Kim's "How Many Licks,"
      and Miss Kim, you are not singing about throwing punches,
but for a while I don't notice because my husband
      is talking about where we will eat dinner, but like a bullet
the lyrics penetrate the armor of the city, the fresco, the tagliata
      and punterelle I'll eat later, and I'm crossing my legs twice,
once at the knees and then at the ankles, but what do I know,
      because my dad never threw me out of the house,
and I've never lived on the streets, and your life, Kim, is like an opera,
      Lucia di Lammermoor maybe, but you're not taking Enrico's shit,
and when Edgardo breaks into your phony wedding you grab him
      and run off to Paris but not before you sing the mad scene,
because what's *Lucia* without it, all the blood and tattoos, and you
      could never sing Mimi, because she's such a simp. No, Musetta's
your gal, so Lil' Kim put on your Queen of the Night gown,
      the corset and headpiece with shooting stars, or your Lulu rags,
Jack the Ripper leading her to his knife, or your Lil' Kim hot pants,
      but remember, Kim, we girls need some secrets while we fix
our lipstick, straighten our push-up bras and little black dresses,
      because we are riding the lonely streets in taxis, limos,
buses, and sports cars, hair a little messy, dying for the night to open up
      dark and mysterious like a song only time can sing.

Reading Can Kill You

My husband and I are at a restaurant with another couple,
        and after a few drinks the other man and I are talking
about how much we love *The Master and Margarita*,
        a novel we've both read many times in different translations,
but it soon becomes apparent his wife and my husband are stewing,
        as if Bob and I had discovered we had a former lover
in common, let's say a woman, and we were more passionate
        about her than our spouses because she was Russian,
and instead of No, she said *Nyet*, which sounds like a sexier *Yes*,
        and Yes was *Da*, which is so much more *Yes* than *Yes*
but with a twinge of *Nyet*, and it was winter, a freezing Siberian
        blizzard with days that began at ten and ended at two,
and we sat in the dark next to the blazing enamel stove
        and for breakfast drank tea from the samovar sweetened
with jam and talked about Gogol's sentences and Mandelstam's
        despair, and then at night it would be love and vodka,
so when Satan showed up with his entourage, we were borne along
        on his cloud of smoke, joining his diabolical magic show,
flinging roubles into paradise, cuddling at night with his giant cat,
        watching the dawn rise, reciting Pushkin and Akhmatova,
thrilling to Mayakovsky's rants, and in the white nights of summer
        we became poetry, every breath an iamb, our cries of ecstasy
the *Nyet* that is *Da*, and I can see why my husband is silent and sulky,
        so I return to our table, sip my Sancerre, talk about Paris,
because all four can agree we'd rather be lost in that city
        than be found in another, and the steppes recede,
but in the middle of my oysters I think of my great grandfather,
        who worked in the mines of Kentucky, and one night
was supposed to be watching the furnace, but he was reading,
        and the furnace exploded, killing him, which led my mother

to threaten that all my reading would destroy me, too, and I pictured

my teenaged self in that dank little room, the fire roaring,

reading a newspaper, a union tract, "Kubla Khan," or maybe

Thomas Hardy's *Far from the Madding Crowd*, whose heroine,

Bathsheba Everdene, was so rich and beautiful and stupid

I could hardly be blamed for not wanting to be anyone but her.

17 Dollars

That's how much the man who owned DuBey's gave me
        for my books that time you insisted
they were taking up space and we needed the money.
        We were poor, sure—you a painter,
me a student—but 17 dollars? I remember looking at it—
        a ten, a five, and two ones—and thinking
how little it was compared to the cardboard box
        you'd lugged into the store that afternoon,
all the days and nights those people—Russian aristocrats,
        English ladies, Southern dingbats, Irish wild men—
taught me how to be human: flawed, yes, but with aspirations
        of divinity. Where were Prince Myshkin,
Dorothea Brooke, Hazel Motes, Stephen Dedalus?
        We could maybe buy groceries for a week
or go to the café down the street for dinner or lunch,
        but how could I get by without my Borges
or *Wuthering Heights*? When I think back on that day,
        that's when my heart hardened in my chest
like a walnut gone bad, so when another man
        told me he loved me, I looked at him
and didn't ask myself would he love me forever
        but would he love my piles of books.
When they began to grow by the bed, teeter on every table,
        and topple to the floor, would his mouth
become thin and his voice rise like an accountant's
        with a ledger? I handed you the money
and walked away. You ran to catch up,
        said, "We can take it back," but I felt
like the poor mother who has given her child
        to the rich couple because they can buy her

frilly dresses, give her piano lessons, send her to fancy schools.

I couldn't take care of my Jane Eyre,

Molly Bloom, Anna Karenina, but maybe someone else could.

Even now I go to my shelves to look for *The Trial*

or *The Day of the Locust* or *Thus Spake Zarathustra*,

and when I can't find them, I know

they were in that box. What did we do after? Walk home,

eat dinner at the cheap Chinese place,

where you picked the shrimp out of eggrolls and asked,

"Is that pork? It tastes like pork." Later

a French couple bought the building, ripped out the red silk

dragons, the lanterns with gold tassels

and turned it into the bistro my new husband and I went to

most weekends when we were first married,

where I learned to drink wine, eat escargots and bitter greens.

Now it's the parking lot of the federal courthouse,

and I can't drink red wine without sneezing. Why did I keep

The Manifestos of Surrealism, which I haven't opened

in thirty years? Where are *The Moviegoer, Nightwood,*

Tender Buttons, Wise Blood? Years later,

both married to other people, you said you were sorry

for making me sell those books. We were standing outside

your studio in Chicago. It was summer and you were holding

your daughter's hand, and I said it was nothing,

but even that day long ago I knew it was everything and it was.

Ode to Red and Speedy

"Bernice," says my mother when I ask her who sent
       the Christmas card signed *Red and Speedy*,
and fifty years later I ask her if Bernice was Red or Speedy,
       and she says, "I don't know," her voice like a raspy
accordion, but I wait till she warms up, and then she starts
       singing, so I learn that even though Bernice
had red hair, she was probably Speedy, because she
       never stopped, unlike my father, her younger brother,
who was perhaps one of the most relaxed people ever to live
       outside a Buddhist monastery, but his sister
was in motion, loved buying houses and remodeling them,
       by profession a beautician, her dark auburn hair
in a perfect French twist, and she always drove a Buick,
       often coordinating the colors of her outfits
with her cars, sometimes convertibles, which led to filmy
       chiffon scarves of baby blue or sea green.
But who was Red? "Maybe that was the one she married
       for a few weeks," my mother says. "She had seven
husbands, her first when she was 13 or 14." When I was ten,
       Bernice and her current husband visited us,
and all I remember was her slim gray suit, a frothy pink dicky
       at the neck. I'd never seen anything so elegant
in my born-again household. There's a photo of Bernice
       in her twenties at a carnival with a caption that reads
Feeling No Pain. Later she became a Bible-wielding
       Christian, to the dismay of her final husband,
a former low-level mafioso from Miami who was famous
       for burying thousands of dollars in coffee cans
but not sealing them and digging up the loot to find the bills
       had rotted. "Wait a minute," my mother says, "maybe

Bernice was Red," and I think of all my nicknames: Miss Astor,
        Mole, Coco, Babster, Dharma Belle, or was it Bell?
Who can remember all the selves stuffed into the miraculous
        sack of skin? Her full name was Bernice Minerva,
a glorious moniker coined by my grandfather, who was murdered
        when my dad was five and Bernice ten. There's a photo
of him looking like Rasputin, and here's a panorama of Bernice's
        seven grooms, nameless now but who lived
in Technicolor once upon a time, and someone finds a photo
        of me and you fifty years from now without a caption,
so here's to Red and Speedy, whoever you were.

Ode to the *Messiah,* Thai Horror Movies, and Everything I
Can't Believe

When I decide to go to hear Handel's *Messiah* in London
      at the composer's parish church, my husband says
he'd rather see a Thai horror movie, so we plan to meet later
      at our favorite Moroccan lair that serves huge platters
of olives and fried goat brains, but here I am sitting in the pew
      next the president of the Handel Society, who tells me
I've taken the seat of his wife who has another engagement,
      and I see her sitting next to my husband watching
Shimabam Rampapoolajib rip the throat of a nubile virgin,
      then run through a seedy bar in Bangkok
and down an alley way to the Chao Phraya River,
      much like the river of music flowing over me,
and the president of the Handel Society explains that in England
      they stand for the Hallelujah chorus, and I assure him
we Yanks do, too, and I think of the last time I heard this music
      I was with my mother in Honolulu and we both stood
as hundreds of voices soared over us like the gods exhaling
      a golden brew of divine moonshine, but here in London
the chorus is only 20 voices, like a group of friends whispering
      the secret to each other and maybe I'm wrong
about the Thai movie, because I'm often wrong about almost everything,
      for example politics—I can't believe my mother
continues to vote against her own best interests because her father,
      dead over 50 years, voted that way, and why do people
have multiple sex partners because everyone knows about germs,
      not to mention *Staphylococcus,* fungus, MRSA, nits,
river blindness, and Ebola, and maybe the flying monsters
      over Bangkok are more moving than sitting in this church
where the great musician sat and listened to his glorious aria,
      "I know that my Redeemer liveth," and though I don't believe

those stories anymore than I believe in Mothra over Tokyo, I do believe
in the notes swimming over me like a river of fireflies
on a summer evening, and when the concert is over I say goodbye
to my new friend, who during the intermission
introduced me to all his friends, men in three-piece pinstriped suits
and tidy haircuts, and I walk out into the December evening,
and if there isn't a flurry of snow there should be, and I am so alone
in this chilly night walking to the Oxford tube stop,
and I would love to see Satan bursting through the starry firmament,
but there are no stars, only a stew of fog, and let's face it
all our monsters are bivouacked in our chests like dyspeptic soldiers
in a mercenary army, hungry, covered in warts
or contagion of some kind, too walleyed and stupid to see
they are flesh and blood and there's a glorious song
somewhere inside waiting to be sung in a church or an opera house
or even a pub where One-Eyed Walter is playing an accordion,
while a drunk warbles on a rusty flute, and Janet, the scullery maid,
her sweet soprano like a tiny bird, fluttering out
of a corner so dark it might be mistaken for an entrance to hell.

Ode to the Triple

Valium, Librium, and Tylenol with codeine—that's what Velma
     the head nurse at the Florida House of Representatives
would dish out when you came in with your period, a hangover,
     a cold, a broken arm, a hangnail. She called it the Triple,
as in *It sounds like you need a Triple* or *That calls for a Triple.*
     God, the Triple was beautiful. You could do your job,
but instead of sitting at your squalid Bartleby desk
     and turning into a cockroach while proofreading
legislative bills commending beauty queens and putting potheads
     in prison, you would be floating on a cloud so silvery
that the words were a kind of neo-beatnik Dadaist poetry,
     and our goddess was Velma, a chunky bleached blonde,
who knew what was going on, so you couldn't show up every day
     or even every week, unless you were a big shot
representative from Palatka, say, or Steinhatchee or Miami Lakes
     in a sherbet-colored polyester leisure suit. Oh, they could
go in any time they wanted and get a quadruple Triple,
     or so we in the proofreading pool fantasized,
because we needed a Triple to get from eight o'clock to lunch,
     when we were released from our cubicles
for sixty minutes, which seemed like sixty seconds, and Cindy
     used to say she wanted them to pay her every hour,
just pop the bills and change down on her desk,
     so when she got fed up she could walk out with her cash
and never come back, and we couldn't imagine someone
     staying at a job so long they could retire, but Velma retired,
and the party was like an inauguration, because everyone
     who was anyone was there and plenty of nobodies, too,
stiff flower arrangements, and a bowl of orange juice and ginger ale
     punch, and then she was gone like a dream,

and the new nurse was doling out plain Tylenol, which changed
        nothing, in fact made it worse, because when your head
or uterus calmed down, you'd go back to the trenches
        and wait to be blown apart by a German howitzer
or chewed by rats, so those of us who were able to escape
        might be forgiven for asking how it happened that one day
the door to that particular realm of hell opened and then closed
        behind us, much the way Burt Lancaster's hands gripped
Tony Curtis's in *Trapeze* when he did the triple somersault
        in the air or Babe Ruth's as he clenched the bat
and hit a home run with the bases loaded, but sometimes
        I find myself saying, "Velma, I need a Triple,"
and she comes down like a Caravaggio angel and pops them
        in my mouth and for a couple of hours I feel
as if I could do anything if only I knew what that could possibly be.

Ode to Wasting Time and Drawing Donatello's *David*

Of all the time I've wasted my favorite has to be the hours
   I've spent drawing Donatello's *David* in the Bargello,
once the Medici prison in Florence, now the sculpture gallery
   and I'm not talking about the marble *David*
with all his clothes on but the naked bronze pretty boy
   wearing only boots and a wide-brimmed hat
with a garland of flowers on the brim; yes, it's with him
   I'm filling notebooks—heads, torsos, full-body drawings,
quick sketches, from every angle. Hey, girls, sketching
   is a great way to pick up guys, a useless bit
of knowledge since I have a handsome husband I'm gaga about,
   but it might be of some help to you, my sisters,
because I was drawing *David* one day when Ron from the UK
   showed me his sketches, *David*, of course,
and a great one he'd done on a bus in Rome, and his line
   was a little heavier than mine, but the drawings
had lots of verve or *sprezzatura*, as the Italians would say,
   and then there was bespeckled Malcolm
from New York who just kept edging up, so I showed him
   my *David*, which Penelope, my drawing teacher,
told me to do. "People are going to look, so just get used to it."
   I have notebooks filled with drawings
of the Alhambra, Japanese pagodas, Italian piazzas, Alabama
   cross gardens and for what? I'm no good
with landscapes and not much better with faces,
   but I always start with the eyebrows—bushy,
arched, pale or dark, the Frieda Kahlos, John L. Lewises—
   and then the nose—aquiline, snub, pinched
or potato, and I'm working on hands—ah, the gorgeous hands
   of Frans Hals—fondling a dog, holding a sword,

plucking a lute, tipping over a glass, hand on heart, fist

on fat waist of pewter taffeta, gloved hand

holding a glove—will I ever plumb the depths of your mystery?

Probably not, just as I will never understand

why I love to read about golf, because I don't play,

have never watched a game on TV, don't know

the rules, but I love to read about the big money tournaments,

the wacky players, the gods and goddesses

of the 18 holes, and what is love anyway but an unexplainable

infatuation that turns into a living creature

you find yourself sleeping beside, eating dinner with

and talking about what you read in the newspapers,

which are a double-tiara royal waste of time, but I read

two every day and talk about art shows in Barcelona,

plays in New York, restaurants in London, the peccadillos

of local politicians with my husband,

who when I first met him looked more like Michelangelo's

David than Donatello's, and he doesn't play golf

or draw, but he does wait for me while I sketch a Van Gogh

self-portrait with pastels or a café tabletop

with black ink or a cat in a window or my own feet,

wasting time in his own way but then, of course,

his name is David or, as they pronounce it in Italy, *DAH-vee-day*,

slayer of Goliath, lover of Bathsheba, poet

of the Psalms, *the Lord is my shepherd, I shall not want*,

a bronze boy with a giant's head resting under his foot.

On the Street of Divine Love

I'm walking down the *Vincolo del Amore Divino* in Rome
        with a girl I hardly know, behind us the Spanish Steps,
Keats's words swimming inside me like thousands of fish
        in a transparent tank of skin, and if his breath lingered,
it's gone now, mixed with the *sieg heils* of Mussolini,
        the ecumenical denunciations of 15 popes, the pidgin
of the Japanese American soldiers from Hawaii
        who liberated Rome but weren't allowed to march into the city
during the day, the cries of the baffled Romans who saw them
        and shouted, *Cinese, Cinese,* and the millions of tourists
aiming cameras with lenses the size of a whale's penis
        saying to the mystified ticket sellers, *Is this a museum?*
What isn't a museum? My body being Exhibit A. Step right up,
        ladies and gents, a once beautiful specimen
broken down by Time and *vino rosso.* I have a lion's teeth
        and a mockingbird's tongue, 400 million items
clogging my curio cabinet brain, and no strategy to clear the clutter.
        Oh, no, my dear doctor, I am adding to the detritus,
as when watching an infomercial at three in the morning, and a woman
        has cured herself of a horrible disease with a ten-point program:
eating organic and drinking more water, yoga, fresh air,
        but the one that really throws me is to forgive everyone
who has ever done me wrong, which I know is right but so very hard to do,
        and I go through all my enemies and wish them well,
but that's not the same as forgiving them, because wishing them well
        is in the future whereas forgiveness is anchored in the past,
which is a continent of jungles, the Gobi Desert, and London bombed
        by the blitz, or so I'm thinking while walking in Rome,
and we pass a shop of gowns so frothy and pink that wearing them
        would transfer you to another plane of existence,

as in a few days when a tsunami will rage through the Indian Ocean,
     and Katrina is in the offing, but of all the gods, Jehovah
must sometimes show his wrath, for he is a jealous god,
     as is Shiva stirring up his mayhem in the waters of Earth,
but I'm walking down the street of divine love,
     Il Vincolo del Amore Divnino, and I want a God
big enough to love those who don't believe in him,
     because isn't it enough just to walk this world
with its psychedelic wah wah, its lightning storms and squalor,
     Paris and Calcutta, so I'm walking down the street of divine love,
listening to Son House sing "John the Revelator"—*Who's that writing?*
     John the Revelator. Who's that writing? It's Rimbaud
on his drunken boat, Noah railing on his ark, the Emperor Domitian
     staging naval battles in the flooded Piazza Navona,
and yesterday I saw Caravaggio's *St. Matthew and the Angel*,
     the otherworldly creature dipping down to tap
the former tax collector on his noggin with some divine inspiration.
     Where is my angel? For I'm on the street of divine love,
and if this pavement isn't God, then I have nothing to pin my hopes on
     like a big orchid corsage before the senior prom, so I am walking,
with the Visigoths rampaging through Rome, *gli fascisti*
     being harangued by Mussolini, popes lining up like Barbie dolls
on Bernini's loggia, Severn burying his friend out by the pyramid
     beyond Rome's walls, where some ragged bird is perched
on a palm tree, singing his heart out for everyone walking alone
     through the alleys and fields of this broken night on Earth.

Ode to Augurs, Ogres, Acorns, and Two or Three Things That Have Been Eating at My Heart Like a Wolverine in a Time of Famine

So many birds are flying above my house it must mean
            something or how could the Romans
have built their roads and cities based on the movement
            of sparrows and falcons in the sky above
the Capitoline Hill, Caesars asking the augurs
            when they should cross the Rubicon, poison their wives,
conquer Asia Minor, and as geese cut across my sky in a sharp *V*
            or starlings swarm into the church tower at sunset
I can see how the Etruscans and later the Romans would look
            to the clouds and these last remnants of the dinosaurs
to help them make their way in the world, so I believe in birds
            as I believe in the mad woman on my street in Florence
who lifts her skirt to show her stuff to anyone
            who won't look away, or Merchino,
the tall gaunt man with a short torso who stalks down
            the Borgo la Croce like a savage medieval prince covered
with tattoos, and when he passes me as I leave our apartment
            or walk through the market, I feel as if he is pulling
the moment in a swirling tornado above his head,
            lifting me in its wake like a magician, though Fabio
tells me he has done time for armed robbery, which is a kind
            of sorcery in itself, evil magi of the *passeggiata*,
when Italians walk out before dinner arm in arm, boys with boys,
            girls with girls, couples old and middle aged,
all in the dying light. Or think of last fall when the three oak trees
            in our yard rained down a plague of acorns, pummeling
our roof all night as if a Nazi panzer division had popped through
            the fabric of time, though their bullets less malign,

and the squirrels so roly-poly that the cats could finally dream
      of catching them as Pharaoh dreamed of the seven fat cows
and the seven lean cows, foretelling the seven years of plenty
      and the seven years of famine, so what do the acorns mean
in their mysterious plentitude, if anything, because the world
      can trick you, as when I was driving toward New Orleans
on I-10, and in the gloaming the semis were bearing down
      on my little white Toyota as if they were ogres
from a fairy tale—giant, muscular killing machines, gobbling
      up everything in their path, though most of the drivers
were probably thinking about dinner or Kansas or turning the garage
      into a sunroom, so maybe the sparrows and acorns
are just sparrows and acorns and the glorious inhabitants
      of the streets around Santa Croce are not magis
and hag goddesses, though as I walk down the cobblestone
      street and the light casts its spell over the city
I seem to see something on the edges of my vision,
      a wolverine-masked earth sprite running
along the edges of any path I take as the sun sets in the dark
      woods. There's Leonardo trudging up Monte Cassine
to test his flying machine, Dante skulking away to Ravenna,
      all our crashes and exiles tearing at our hearts
like wild animals reminding us how far we are from home.

I'm Making Walt Whitman Soup

Which is what I call chicken soup, because once I got
        blood poisoning cooking up a pot—raw chicken,
nick from a knife, the next day a puffy thumb, then blue streaks
        running up my arm like an evil river in my own veins,
fever, delirium—and I was reading *Specimen Days* at the time,
        about Whitman's Civil War nursing and how robust
his health was before he got blood poisoning assisting
        with an operation and how he never really recovered,
and when I'm telling my friend Bob this, he asks
        if reading about Whitman's blood poisoning alerted me
to mine, and I said, "No, I think it caused it," because reading
        will do that to you if you don't watch out, like the time
I was reading *The Idiot*, and I saw that my boyfriend was playing me
        like Gavril Ivolgin was playing the gorgeous messed-up
Nastasya Filippovna, who was playing him right back,
        so maybe that's not a very good example. Let's try again—
my beloved Dorothea Brooke—when she married Mr. Causabon
        and he turned out to be a horror show on ice skates,
I realized my next boyfriend was not the incarnation of Krishna
        he claimed to be but was writing *The Key to All Mythologies*,
so which came first—the chicken or the lightning bolt to the third eye?
        But back to the Civil War—what a mess, like any war
with young men being used as cannon fodder, and here we are
        in the middle of three wars with another civil war
brewing between the coasts and heartland, and I remember
        being stopped by a woman in Milan who said
how beautiful the city was before we bombed it to ashes,
        and now we were bombing Iraq and Afghanistan. Her face
was trembling and I wished I'd had the Italian to say, Signora,
        how beautiful we all were before the bombs fell on our frescoes,

on the young men who should have been holding their sweethearts
instead of maiming each other at Chickamauga
and Gettysburg, on every song that rises from our throats.

Questions for My Body

Your brain's like 100 million hornets in a Campbell's Soup can,
        so where's the axe to split it open?
Speaking of can openers, what is it about midnight that makes
        your spine shake like the hand of a holy roller
        shooting craps against a back alley curb?
        Click, click, click—snake eyes, and all your pretty dresses
        lie in tatters, Ave Maria and her butternut squash.
Why do some days seem like factory work and others like a picnic
        at the beach? What's in the picnic basket—fried chicken?
Is that the same chicken nesting in your throat, with her
        tambourine and Old Testament phlegm? Glory
        be to God in the highest. Roll over Rover, let Jimi take over.
How can your heart be as hard as the face of Teddy Roosevelt
        on Mount Rushmore and as soft as the stomach
        of the fat boy on the bus, crust of chocolate around his mouth?
And where did you get your nasty mouth? In that pile of body parts
        behind the morgue?
Götterdämmerung, girlfriend, are you speaking in tongues—is that why
        you dream about running away to Mexico? Do you want
        to blame your mental riot on not speaking Spanish?
Si, si señora, remember when you were first married, and every time
        you wore a loose shirt, someone would squeal,
        "Are you going to have a baby?" Did you have to say,
        "I'd love to, but their heads are so big and my vagina's so small?"
How did you sharpen your tongue? With that missing ax,
        or did you use a matchbook from the Pair-o-Dice Lounge?
        Remember the years you walked down that blind alley?
        There's no scrapbook to hold those photos.
Why do *sex* and *hex* rhyme? What about Tex-Mex? Cerebral cortex?
        Why is sex like eating at a Mexican restaurant—beans and rice,
        tequila, habañeros—¡Ay, caramba!
O my darling mumbojumbologist, who is the architect of your double talk?

Who made you from her bones and bread?

Will you never stop missing your mother's voice?

Did you know that Hindus believe we are God experiencing himself?

Does that make you a holy chalice or a holy chassis?

O Chevy Vishnu, Studebaker Jesus. O Buick Bodhisattva
of the Bebop-a-lou.

Why does luck make you feel like you're in front of a firing squad,
looking down the barrels of 14 rifles? You think
you're Dostoevsky, don't you?

That reminds me, why are you so in love with Prince Myshkin? Don't you
remember he lost his mind? Do you want to lose your mind?
Don't you wish it were that easy?

If you could go back in time, who would you save—Keats? Marlowe?
Carole Lombard? Okay, so you could talk Lombard out of getting
on that plane, ditto Buddy Holly and Otis Redding, but how
would you get the penicillin back to Keats? And how good
would a sissy girl like you be in a knife fight?

Remember that Tootsie Roll you ate when you were 12? You should.
It's still on your left hip.

So why do you bother to get out of bed in morning?

Because last time you checked your name wasn't Marcel Proust.

Because like Samuel Beckett, you've been waiting all your life
to be old.

Because a nickel will get you a shoe shine, but a penny will get
you the nothing that is so something else.

Because there's no business like show business.

Because being an animal is so shambolic.

Because you're stuck here like a cluck-mad chicken on the wrong
side of the road, Tom Joad on amphetamines, high queen
of spleen, trying to outfox your ultra-sneaky archenemy
that teetotaling Mr. T, two-timing Time

DELIRIUM

(1995)

The language of bees contains 76 distinct words for stinging,
       distinguishes between a prick, puncture, and mortal wound,
elaborates on cause and effect as in a sting made to retaliate,
       irritate, insinuate, infuriate, incite, rebuke, annoy,
       nudge, anger, poison, harangue.
The language of bees has 39 words for queen—regina apiana,
       empress of the hive, czarina of nectar, maharani of the ovum,
       sultana of stupor, principessa of dark desire.

The language of bees includes 22 words for sunshine,
Two for rain—big water and small water, so that a man urinating
       on an azalea bush in the full fuchsia of April
       has the linguistic effect of a light shower in September.
For man, two words—roughly translated—"hands" and "feet,"
       the first with the imperialistic connotation of beekeeper,
       the second with the delicious resonance of bareness.
All colors are variations on yellow, from the exquisite
       sixteen-syllable word meaning "diaphanous golden fall,"
       to the dirty ochre of the bitter pollen
       stored in the honeycomb and used by bees for food.

The language of bees is a language of war. For what is peace
       without strife but the boredom of enervating day-after-day,
       obese with sweetness, truculent with ennui?
Attack is delightful to bees, who have hundreds of verbs
       embracing strategy, aim, location, velocity:
       swift, downward swoop to stun an antagonist,
       brazen, kamikaze strike for no gain but momentum.
Yet stealth is essential to bees, for they live to consternate
       their enemies, flying up pant legs, hovering in grass.

No insect is more secretive than the bee, for they have two
        thousand words describing the penetralia of the hive:
        octagonal golden chamber of unbearable moistness,
        opaque tabernacle of nectar,
        sugarplum of polygonal waxy walls.

The language of bees is a language of aeronautics,
        for they have wings—transparent, insubstantial,
        black-veined like the fall of an exotic iris.
For they are tiny dirigibles, aviators of orchard and field.
For they have ambition, cunning, and are able to take direct aim.
For they know how to leave the ground, to drift, hover, swarm,
        sail over the tops of trees.

The language of bees is a musical dialect, a full, humming
        congregation of hallelujahs and amens,
        at night blue and disconsolate,
        in the morning bright and bedewed.
The language of bees contains lavish adjectives
        praising the lilting fertility of their queen:
        fat, red-bottomed progenitor of millions,
        luscious organizer of coitus,
        gelatinous distributor of love.
The language of bees is in the jumble of leaves before rain,
        in the quiet night rustle of small animals,
        for it is eloquent and vulgar in the same mouth,
        and though its wound is sweet it can be distressing,
        as if words could not hurt or be meant to sting.

Betrothal in B minor

All women bewail the betrothal of any woman,
beamy-eyed, bedazzled, throwing a fourth finger

about like a marionette. Worse than marriage
in many ways, an engagement, be it moments or millennia,

is a morbid exercise in hope, a mirage, a romance
befuddled by magazine photographs of lips, eyebrows,

brassieres, B-cups, bromides, bimbos bedaubed
with kohl, rouged, bespangled, beaded, beheaded,

really, because a woman loses the brain
she was born with if she believes for a moment

she of all women will escape enslavement of mind,
milk, mooring, the machinations of centuries,

to arrive in a blissful, benign, borderless
Brook Farm where men are uxorious, mooning,

bewitched, besotted, bereft of all beastly,
beer-guzzling qualities. Oh, no, my dear

mademoiselle, marriage is no *déjeuner sur l'herbe*,
no bebop with Little Richard for eternity,

no bedazzled buying spree at Bergdorf or Bendel,
no clinch on the beach with Burt Lancaster

although it is sometimes all these things, it is
more often, to quote la Marquise de Merteuil, "War,"

but war against the beastliness within that makes
us want to behave, eat beets, buy beef at the market,

wash with Fab, betray our beautiful minds
tending to the personal hygiene of midgets.

My God, Beelzebub himself could not have manufactured
a more Machiavellian maneuver to bedevil an entire

species than this benighted impulse to replicate
ourselves ad nauseam in the confines of a prison

so perfect bars are redundant. Even in the Bible
all that begetting and begatting only led to misery,

morbidity, Moses, and murder. I beseech you,
my sisters, let's cease, desist, refrain,

take a breather, but no one can because we are
driven by tiny electrical sparks that bewilder,

befog, beguile, becloud our angelic intellect.
Besieged by hormones, we are stalked by a disease

unnamed, a romantic glaucoma. We are doomed to die,
bespattered and besmirched beneath the dirt,

under the pinks and pansies of domestic domination.
Oh, how I loathe you—perfect curtains, exquisite chairs,

crème brûlée of my dreams. Great gods of pyromania,
begrudge not your handmaiden, your fool, the flames

that fall from your fiery sky, for my dress is tattered
and my shoes are different colors, blue and red.

Ova

Oval, hard-shelled or soft, eaten for breakfast,
bought in dozens, six to a row, two rows, brown or white,

subject of riddles (which came first), subject of fables,
to wit the goose and the golden one, symbol of Christ

in Piero della Francesca's sublime painting in which he
suspends an ostrich's over the impassive sphere

of the Virgin's head, not that the attendant angels
with their buttery curls or saints notice, so busy are they

studying the tiles and the shine on Federigo da Montefeltro's
armor and bald head. A chicken lays one at a time,

a fish hundreds, a queen bee mates with a dozen or so drones
and commences to lay them for over a year. And think

of the discrete parts: the shells—is there a more perfect shape
in nature? Certainly not, according to Carl Gustavovich Fabergé,

whose begemmed and enameled concoctions delighted
the hemophilia-carrying scions of the frayed remnants

of imperial Russia; or the white, pellucid, slippery albumen
that, whipped to hysterical heights, becomes meringue,

snowy chapeaux of fruity tarts and pies; and the yolk—
round, golden orb that mixed with water and hue and affixed

to board can become *La Primavera* or *The Birth of Venus*.
Scramble it, bake it, pickle it, fry it—over easy,

sunny-side up. Caviar and champagne, omelet, quiche, frittata.
Everyone emanates from one, little zygotes, piling on one

confusing cell after another but forever beset by an atavistic
longing to be once more oval with a heart of gold.

Toska

I still haven't forgiven Natasha for marrying Pierre,
not actually for marrying him but for being happy with him.

How could she, after Prince Andrei? I know, I know,
life must go on, but I want something finer for her,

beyond wiping snotty noses and hanging on his every word.
Not a modern epilogue with everyone dead or bitterly unhappy

or both, but something else, a sense of longing or ache
for which there is no word in English. In Russian

there is the word *toska*, which describes an undefined desire,
a sense that what you need and want most is elsewhere

or doesn't exist at all. English wouldn't have a word
for such a feeling, for ours is a language of materialism first,

a language in which ideally everything you need is obtainable
because everything can be bought. French is another language

which would probably not have a word like *toska*
though there is the *conditionnel antérieur*, or the tense of regret,

yet regret is not what I want Natasha to feel nor melancholy.
The French word *ennui* is better than *boredom* but still not quite right.

At the Tower of Babel when God first gave us languages,
what was it like? Everyone jabbering like crazy, trying to find

someone who understood what he was saying and then sorting
themselves out? Or was it like being struck by lightning—

nothing the same, bricklayers contemplating their mortar
and not knowing what it was for, much less what it was called?

This seems more likely. I can see people wandering off—
befuddled husbands knowing their wives but not knowing them

at the same time, and friends passing each other and remembering
that they are friends but not knowing what a friend is.

How wonderful it had been for a time, planning the tower,
deciding on its diameter and circumference, the philosophy

of it all. There had even been a delegation whose entire function
was composing a speech to be delivered when they finally

came face to face with God. Alas, these poor pundits
later migrated to a land just north of the Alps and developed

a maddening portmanteau language that when faced with a miracle
such as the Assumption of the Virgin into heaven on a cloud

of angels came up with *Himmelfahrt Maria*, which, though not
precisely untrue, reveals no sense of God as a patriarchal vacuum

or the shock of the Apostles below and their desolation at losing her.
Desolation is a good word, but not what I want for Natasha,

nor is it *toska*, because what she most needed existed once
but is gone as is that inclination to converse with God.

St. Anthony of the Floating Larynx

We take a train to Padua to see the Giottos, lapis and gold,
and the mostly-destroyed Mantegna frescoes of the life

of St. James, blown to bits by a wayward American bomb,
patched together like a puzzle now, but with most pieces missing.

My friend is on a pilgrimage to the Cathedral of St. Anthony
of Padua, patron saint of harvest, lovers, sick animals,

and lost objects, *oggetti* in Italian, and this church
is quite an Oggetto itself, with a capital "O"

and I have seen my share of shrines in the last three months.
Immediately I recognize that this is no ordinary repository

of frescoes, plastic statuary, and other divine bric-a-brac.
It is a hive of religiosity, alive with bizarre reliquaries;

in fact we stand in line to see St. Anthony's larynx, yes indeed,
his voice box, suspended in a gelatinous scarlet liquid,

a cartilaginous snake of animal matter, from which my husband
(educated by Jesuits) turns, white as a piece of typing paper.

This is the Italy I dreamed of, saints, snakes, gypsies,
cutthroats in a baroque tutu of religion and sin.

The venality of it all is like eating cake for breakfast,
though it's obvious that not much cake eating is going on

in the Cathedral of St. Anthony but rather atonement
for cake eating, for three quarters of the multitude in the church

are on their knees, reminding me of a Billy Graham Crusade
I attended as a twelve-year-old when the great man himself said,

"Fall down on your knees and pray for God's forgiveness."
It's an interesting concept, forgiveness, and one, I must say,

that appeals to the throng in Padua, or are they praying
for miracles? In a sense forgiveness is a miracle, or at least

for someone like me who finds pardon difficult and unfulfilling,
or as Mary Ann Wolf used to say, "What good's a grudge

if you can't hold it?" What would St. Anthony have to say about mercy?
I wonder as I queue up with my friend at the saint's tomb.

She wants a husband and I want back the bag that Alitalia
lost three months ago in Rome. As I raise my arm to place my palm on

the wall of the tomb, a four-by-four grandmother dressed
in black cuts in front of me and knocks my arm out of the way.

Her problem is probably a lot more pressing than a suitcase
of dresses, which, by the way, St. Anthony delivers to me

a month later in the Miami airport. My friend is still single,
although her old boyfriend called and told her she was

the love of his life, not exactly her dream come true
but in the true-love ballpark. Maybe the saints do better

with material requests. A green silk dress has got to be easier
to deliver than a boyfriend with a job and a working personality.

Metaphysics is so tiring, which is what St. Anthony would probably
say if he could, lying in that tomb, sans larynx, teeth,

and assorted other body parts. Day after day, we line up with our
problems, raise our troubled palms. "Maria? No, my friend, she's

wrong for you. It won't last more than a year." And the poor guy
goes off, thinking, That Maria, I could really be happy with her.

St. Clare's Underwear

You can see why men are such monsters when you look
at a woman's body, Devonshire creamy from a bath,

or just the general curviness of the whole design. Then
there's your average man, hirsute and raging with testosterone,

Godzilla *incarnato*, King Kong with big feet, Frankenstein
hovering over some delectable damsel with skin like fresh pastry.

So you can see why St. Clare threw in her lot with St. Francis,
a nice guy, good with animals, although there were rumors.

But aren't there always? In Italian, the word for noise is *rumore*,
which is what gossip is, though why women should be thought

more inclined to tittle-tattle than men is a mystery to me,
but not something I was thinking about one evening in Florence

as my husband and I strolled along the Lungarno Soderini
and in the Piazza Cestello happened upon a theater presenting

Goldoni's *The Gossip of Women*, though after one act I felt
that it could have as easily been called *The Foppery of Men*.

My dear, the prancing and smirking that transpired,
and in a country known for its machismo. When the young lover

puckered his carmine lips, the men in the audience
were making a noise that sounded for all the world like laughter,

though one can never be certain. I learned something that night,
though exactly what, I'm not sure, and my education continued

in Assisi where we saw glass cases with the clothes of St. Francis
and St. Clare, sandals and sackcloth, though Clare's case

contained what looked like a rough slip or chemise. "St. Clare's
underwear," I cried with such happiness to my husband,

but at that point he was sick of me and my non-Catholic
lack of respect for everything he no longer holds dear.

In Italy you are either *cattolico* or *acattolico*, which, I imagine,
makes Anglicans and Four-Square Gospel Pentecostals

rather uneasy bed partners, as, I suppose, hermaphrodites
and transsexuals are made anxious by the words "woman"

and "man." I like to think of Kierkegaard's idea of the natural home
of despair being in the "heart of happiness," which could mean

any number of things, such as black is not black or even white,
or that we are all as confused as Dracula, dreaming

of a local milkmaid, her C-cup, coarse lingerie, ruddy cheeks,
and the blood, of course, always the blood.

Nose

I am trying on an especially evil-looking pair of shoes
when the shopgirl points to the middle of her face and says,

"This is called what?" For a moment I draw a blank as I search
my mind for the Italian word for snoot, schnozzola, beak,

but when "il naso" finally surfaces, I realize
that she is Italian and probably knows the Italian word

for nose, so what she wants is the English,
which is relatively easy for me, so I say, "Nose."

"Nose," she replies, smiling. "You have a beautiful nose."
I am looking at the shoes on my feet. I have dangerous feet,

especially in these particular shoes, but my nose
is rather white bread, too much like my skinflint grandmother's

for me to ever be entirely ecstatic about it,
and this girl's is spectacular, an aquiline viaduct

spanning the interval from her eyes to her delicious lips.
A friend once told me, "My sister paid $2,000

for a nose like yours, a perfect shiksa nose,
but it ending up looking like Bob Hope's."

Suddenly, I feel as if I have no nose, like Gogol's Kovelev
riding around St. Petersburg looking for his proboscis.

What is a nose? Obviously not simply a smeller, sniffer,
or a mere searcher out of olfactory sensation,

but something more—an aesthetic appendage to the facial
construction, a slope from brow to philtrum,

with symmetrical phalanges. Aren't I precise, who knows
nothing about having an unsatisfactory nose, or ever thinking

about it for one second? Perhaps my offending part
is somewhere else, or am I as hapless as Gogol's hero—

with too little nose for my purposes, like Miss Ruby Diamond,
the richest woman in my town, who lost her nose to cancer,

and had two counterfeits, one lifelike and the other
a simple plastic flap to hide the scar of ninety years.

A nose is a nose is a nose is a nose,
Gertrude Stein did not say and why would she

as it is obviously untrue? Though each nose is an island
in the sea of the face, sticking out in a more or less

inadequate fashion. Like Cyrano, I marshal my couplets,
ragtag though they be, to celebrate all noses unloved,

those lost to disease or, like Kovelev's, inadvertently
misplaced, and the nose of the shopgirl on the Via Roma

in Firenze, her eyes red from either smoking pot or heartbreak
and the many other indignities gathered like humps on our backs,

which we touch for luck, as if floods, bombings, murders
could only happen to others who are beautiful and pure.

Delirium

Just before I fainted in the restaurant that evening,
        I was telling you a story about a madman
        I saw earlier in the day
as I walked home from my ballet class
        just off the Piazza Santa Maria del Carmine.
After crossing the bridge of Santa Trinita,
        looking in at Ghirlandaio's frescoes
        for the Sassetti family,
then wondering how many women there were
        who were young and rich enough
to wear the see-through lace cowboy shirts
        in the Gianni Versace windows
        on the Via Tornabuoni,
at the intersection of the Via de Calzaioli
        and the Via del Corso,
I walked into a hullabaloo being drummed up
        by a bearded man who was stalking back and forth,
screaming something in Italian, of course,
        and waving his arms in the air.
But when he turned he would reach down with one hand,
        clamp his crotch,
        and then pull his body around
as though his hips were a bad dog
        and his genitals a leash he was yanking.
After each turn he'd continue stalking and flailing,
        until time to turn again.
So I am trying to explain this and our pizza comes,
        and I saw off a bite, but it is too hot,
so what do I do but swallow it, and it's too hot,
        and I think, it's too hot,

and my voice decelerates as if it is a recording
       on a slowly melting tape and the scene
       in the restaurant begins to recede:
in the far distance I see the bearded man ranting
       on the street,
then nearer but retreating quickly you
       and the long corridor of the restaurant,
then it's as if I am falling into a cavity behind me,
       one that is always there, though I've learned to ignore it,
but I'm falling now, first through a riot of red rooms,
       then gold, green, blue and darker
       until I finally drift into the black room
       where my mind can rest.
I wake up in the kitchen, lying on a wooden bench,
       with you and the waiter staring at me.
"I'm fine," I say, though it's as if I am pulling
       my mind up from a deep well.
The waiter brings me a bowl of soup,
       which I don't want, but it doesn't matter because
the lights go out and a man at the next table says,
       "Primo quella signora ed ora la luce,"
which means, first that woman and now the light,
       and it's so dark that I can't see myself or you,
and I feel as if I'm turning, a mad voice
       rising from my stomach
crying where are we anyway, and who, and what, and why?

THE ALPHABET OF DESIRE

(1999)

The Word

In the beginning was the word, fanning out into syllables
        like a deck of cards on a table in Vegas,
litigious leafy parts fluttering into atoms and cells,
        genus and phylum, nouns, verbs,
elephants, orangutans, O Noah, you and your philological
        filing and filling of arks, gullets, daughters.
In the beginning was the word and it was as big
        as Aretha Franklin after "Chain of Fools,"
long as your mother's memory of all your misdeeds,
        wide as Jerusalem, a fat-lady-in-the-circus word,
a Siberia, a steppe, a savanna, a stretch, a Saturnalia,
        the party at the end of the world.
In the beginning was the word and we knew which way it went:
        left to right in English, right to left
in Hebrew, an orientation so profound that sexual climax
        is coming in all right-moving languages
going in those advancing left, though in the moment
        we rarely know whether we're coming or going.
In the beginning was the word, small and perfect,
        a Hans Holbein miniature, a dormouse,
a gnat, a bee, a blink, a breath in the lungs
        of Jehovah, Brahman, the Buddha, Ra,
because all the big kahunas of the universe surfed
        in on the crest of that first wave,
and Thomas Edison said let there be light
        and the dinosaurs groaned in their graves,
and there was Albuquerque, late-night roadhouses,
        blues, cigarettes, fish-net stockings,
high-density sodium street lights that blot out the stars,
        cars, diners, the neon urban carnival before Lent,

and Marie Curie said let there be more light,

      and there was radium, radiant thermonuclear

incandescent explosions, Herr Einstein's dream,

      Herr Oppenheimer's furnace,

London burning with Hitler's fire, Dresden cremated

      in the answering flame, Hiroshima mon amour.

I ask you, what is this world with its polyglot delirium,

      its plain-spoken, tight-assed, stumble-bum euphoria?

Explain time, for I am fretting on the outskirts of Odessa,

      with Chekhov, with Eisenstein, with ten thousand

martyrs of unremembered causes, and we are cold, hungry,

      tired of playing Hearts.

Where are you, my minister of *informazione*, Comrade Surgeon,

      Mister Wizard, Gino Romantico?

Can you in your lingo ferret out the first word? Inspect

      your dialect for clues, my Marlowe, my Holmes,

your patois for signs, your pagan vernacular, your scatological

      cant, your murmuring river of carnal honey,

for in the beginning there was darkness until you came,

      my pluperfect anagram of erotic delight,

my wild-haired professor of vinissimo and mayhem,

      emperor of Urbino, incubator of rhythm, bright-eyed Apollo

of the late-night bacchanalia, and there was music,

      that heady martini of mathematics and beauty.

For I am empty, I am full, I am certain, I am not,

      for in the beginning there was nothing

and it was blank and indescribable,

      a wave breaking on the north shore of the soul,

but as every canyon aches for its sky, I burned for you

      with a fever, with a frenzy,

I was a woman craving a blaze, a flame,
       a five-alarm fire in my heart, in my bones,
my hair red as a hibiscus, like a burning bush,
       I was Moses screaming at God,
filaments of flame eating my eyes,
       my sex, the hard sweet apple of my mouth.

Thinking of Galileo

When, during a weekend in Venice, while standing
          with the dark sky above the Grand Canal
exploding in arcs of color and light, a man behind me

begins to explain the chemical composition
          of the fireworks and how potassium-something-ate
and sulfur catalyze to make the gold waterfall of stars

cascading in the moon-drunk sky, I begin to understand
          why the Inquisition tortured Galileo
and see how it might be a good thing for people to think

the sun revolves around the earth. You don't have to know
          how anything works to be bowled over by beauty,
but with an attitude like mine we'd still be swimming

in a sea of smallpox and consumption, not to mention plague,
          for these fireworks are in celebration
of the Festival of the Redentore, or Christ the Redeemer,

whose church on the other side of the canal was built
          after the great plague of 1575 to thank him
for saving Venice, though by that time 46,000 were dead,

and I suppose God had made his point if indeed he had one.
          The next morning, Sunday, we take the vaporetto
across the lagoon and walk along the Fondamenta della Croce,

littered with the tattered debris of spent rockets
          and Roman candles, to visit the Church of the Redentore
by Palladio. The door is open for mass, and as I stand in the back,

a miracle occurs: after a year of what seems to be futile study,
      I am able to understand the Italian of the priest.
He is saying how important it is to live a virtuous life,

to help one's neighbors, be good to our families,
      and when we err to confess our sins
and take communion. He is speaking words I know:

vita, parlare, resurrezione. Later my professor tells me
      the holy fathers speak slowly and use uncomplicated
constructions so that even the simple can understand

Christ's teachings. The simple: well, that's me,
      as in one for whom even the most elementary transaction
is difficult, who must search for nouns the way a fisherman

throws his net into the wide sea, who must settle
      for the most humdrum verbs: I am, I have, I go, I speak,
and I see nothing is simple, even my desire to strangle

the man behind me or tell him that some things
      shouldn't be explained, even though they can be,
because most of the time it's as if we are wandering

lost in a desert, famished, delirious, set upon by wild lions
      or plague, our minds blank with fear,
starving for a crumb, for any morsel of light.

The Dream of the Red Drink

This story begins, as they so often do, with heartbreak.
I am at a party for a young man whose wife has left him,
        so he's abandoning graduate school to join the Navy.
There is a lot of despair at this gathering,
        the young man's and the impoverished students'
and, of course, mine, which has less to do with money
        and more to do with time,
which is running out, in case you haven't noticed.
And then there is the red drink.

Our host looks as if he has just stepped out
        of a Trollope novel, a nineteenth-century cleric,
rotund in rumpled chinos and a tee shirt.
        He and a friend have driven to Georgia
to buy grain alcohol and have mixed it with red Kool-Aid
        in a styrofoam container on the back porch.
Later when this party is famous, I learn the red drink
        ate through the styrofoam,
but this was not discovered until the next day
        or maybe the next week when heads had finally cleared.
My host warns me not to drink much.
I don't, but I drink enough.

I don't know anyone at this party but the red drink
        makes me intrepid.
I talk to many people, make jokes, see God.
How many times can you see God before you realize
        his face is different every time?
Is this a revelation? Maybe.
Not only do I see God, but I see through him

to the other side, though probably it's a vision
        of cerebral matter being sloughed off,
and I have a *tête-à-tête* with my most persistent epiphany,
        that is, life is nothing, *rien, nada, niente.*
I find it comforting to know the world is transparent,
        insubstantial, without meaning.
I think of Niels Bohr's assertion that there is no deep
        reality, and I know exactly what he means.
I am looking through the woman I am talking to,
        seeing through her
        to the soft bank of azalea bushes behind.
It's a nice effect, rather like a double exposure.

My husband is at this party, but I am avoiding him
        for a reason I can't really remember.
Oh, I remember, but it's too tedious to go into here.
I look at this man whom I love to distraction
        and wonder how he can be so utterly dense,
and I know if I say anything he will say
        I've had too much to drink, which is entirely correct,
and that there's alcoholism in my family, but show me a family
        that doesn't have a drinker or two. . . .
My beloved is in a cluster of beautiful students
        who think he's marvelous, which he is.
Wait a minute, girls, I could tell you things,
        but the red drink has turned ethereal on me,
and it's two-thirty in the morning and the young man
        who's going into the Navy is delirious or dead,
and the lovely students have disappeared
        into their enchanted student hovels.

So we leave and the car seems flimsy, as if made from
        cardboard, like the East German cars about which
I saw a documentary in a hotel room in Tampa:
        after World War II the East Germans didn't have any steel,
so they made cars out of cotton wool compressed
        between layers of organic plastic
        that has proved to be almost unbiodegradable.
I look out into the night and think, this could be East Berlin,
        except it so obviously isn't, unless magnolias
and enormous oaks dripping with Spanish moss have been sighted
        on the Alexanderplatz.
But we are in motion and I sit in my seat, pulled through
        the night as if by a magnet
to an intersection in which I see that a low-slung black
        Oldsmobile will run a red light
and plow into my side of our flimsy East German car
        and the metaphysical and the physical worlds will have
to come to some kind of decision about my corporeal frame,
        and I think maybe I don't want to walk
        into that good night just yet.

I say to my husband, "That black car's not going to stop,"
and he slows down, even though we have the green light,
        because I have authority in my voice,
authority bestowed on me by the red drink; in fact, I believe
        the red drink has made me psychic,
        because the black car doesn't stop.
We watch it sail through the deserted early-morning
        intersection with wonder and astonishment,
        or at least I do

for Death has passed me by, its chariot zooming toward Perry,

        Florida, driven by a laughing young man with an Elvis

        haircut and his blonde teenaged girlfriend.

Time passes, probably a few minutes, but it seems

        interminable hours have stretched out before us.

We continue through the now empty intersection,

        down an oak-lined street,

and turn to drive through the park,

        but a red fox is in the middle of the rumpled

asphalt and stares into our headlights.

        He has a message for me and for my husband

and the pretty spellbound students

        and our Trollopian host

and the unconscious soon-to-be ensign,

        and I should be able to hear it, but I'm giddy

with being alive, my arms chilled from the sleeve of death.

Achtung, My Princess, Good Night

Arrivederci, Cinderella, your goose is cooked, grilled,
burned to be precise, blistered, while you, nestled in your

crumbling necropolis of love, think, who am I?
Delores del Rio? No, nothing so déclassé, yet

even your mice have deserted you, little pipsqueaks,
fled to serve your stepsisters, dedicated now to

good works, a soup kitchen, if you can imagine. What is this
heresy of ugliness that has overtaken the world?

I am Beauty, you scream. Wrong fairy tale, and
just so you don't forget, size sixes are not enough in this

karaoke culture, and even here you have to do more than
lip sync "Begin the Beguine," "My Funny Valentine,"

"Mona Lisa," "Satisfaction," because you can't get no,
no, no, no, consummation, so to speak. Sex is kaput,

over, married a decade, three litters of princes and
princesses, your figure shot, not to mention your vagina. Don't

quote me on that you cry, my public can't bear very much
reality. Who can? Yet there it is staring you in the face.

Scram, vamoose, la cucaracha, cha cha cha. Admit it, you're
tired of this creepy pedestal, the pressed pleats,

undercooked chicken, Prince Embonpoint and his cheesy
Virna Lisi look-alike mistress with her torpedo chest. Auf

Wiedersehen to this stinking fairy tale life, this pack-rat
Xanadu built on the decomposing carcasses of girlish hope.

Yes, all your best friends, all your gorgeous diamonds are cubic
zirconias, but flashing like the real thing, as if you'd know.

Hatred

Abracadabra, says Mephisto, the firefly
buddha of Rue Morgue, and the whole wide world

changes from a stumbling rick-rack machine
doing the rag time, the bag time, the I'm-on-the

edge-of-a-drag time to a tornado of unmitigated
fury. Yes sir, we are trampling out our vengeance,

grapes-of-wrath time is here again when I think about
Her Majesty, myself, all alone on her throne, tiara askew,

inconsistently worshipped, even by herself, and I could
just die to think how I betray myself in the great

Kabuki theater of my mind, the No Theater, so to speak, but
latitudinal issues aside, here I am starring in a

mystery play. Everyone's in place—cows, shepherds,
no-good-rotten Herod and his ridiculous Roman soldiers.

Only the savior's missing. What's the point, then
putti aside, of the whole big preposterous

Quattrocento mess, the fights, the plague, the frivolous
rococo results, postmodern la-di-da incarnate?

So what's a girl to do when stuck in the last vestiges of the
tawdry twentieth century—have a drink, a fling, say

Uncle? Oh, there's no loathing like self-loathing,
vox populi, vox dei or something like that. I'm rejecting

Western thought here, monotheism included, shuddering as
xenophobic clouds gather over the darkening earth, yeah,

yeah, everyone hates someone, me included, cowering in my
Zen bomb shelter, longing for a thermonuclear whack.

So Long, Roy

Apropos of nothing it seems, I burst into tears on reading
        "Roy Rogers Est Mort," or maybe it's
because I'm living in Paris and homesick or more likely
        that Roy looks just like my dad who's had
cancer three times and lives in Hawai'i, and I'm ten thousand
        miles away and the last time he called, my
dad, not Roy, he sounded tired and confused and not
        at all like the tall,
elegant guy I remember from childhood who erased that image
        as soon as he opened his mouth, speaking
fractured French and making goofy jokes, and I think it must
        be the Cherokee blood
giving them both that heap big handsome cowboy look,
        but what made him laugh after going through
hard knocks right and left, the Depression, dead father,
        careless mother?
Is that why they both turned to religion, stopped calling
        on Jack Daniels, switching to
Jesus? Who wouldn't after seeing a world gone mad,
        the camps, a crazy
kamikaze pilot hitting a ship in my dad's convoy,
        and him watching it sink into the South Pacific
looking on as almost everyone aboard died, most of them still boys
        yanked from factories and farms,
men burning to death or drowning because other men
        wanted to rule the world,
not that any of them succeeded, and after the war my dad
        was stationed
on an island in the Philippines, and because he didn't play
        cards began to read

poetry, memorizing great hunks of it, which he recited
        as my bedtime stories,
quoting "The Shooting of Dan MacGrew," and still doing it
        over the telephone, asking how my students like
Robert Service, and I not having the heart to tell him
        I don't teach
Service but a bunch of feel-bad moderns like Eliot and Pound,
        great lover of Mussolini,
two wretched anti-Semites, who suddenly I see through my dad's
        eyes, which are growing dim,
unfocused except on the past, where he's still a young man,
        his life an adventure, ups and downs,
victories and defeats, moving from Oklahoma to California,
        singing in bands. Go
west, young man, go west to Alaska, Hollywood, Hawai'i,
        marry decent Christian women, pretty women,
excellent women, buy suburban bungalows, father children,
        entertain them with your stories, your poems,
your shows, but for God's sake don't die and let them see your
        photograph in the newspaper, *le journal, die*
Zeitung, so the whole world can remember your smile and how great
        you looked on a horse.

Trigger Tries to Explain

Aw, Dale, he didn't mean it when he said I was the
best thing that ever happened to him. If he even said it,

chalk it up to the RKO publicity machine. I'm a horse, a
dead one at that, mounted in the museum with glass

eyes and looking a little ratty as the tubby former fans
file by with their bewildered bored kids, who are thinking,

Golden palomino, my ass, I can't believe he brought us
here instead of Disneyland, the boys looking like overgrown

insects and the girls like prostitutes in their halter tops,
jean short-shorts and platform sandals. It would have

killed Roy to see them, being such a goody-goody, always
Leonard Slye just beneath the skin with his Oklahoma homilies,

making everyone feel safe and sound. Oh, sure the big bad
Nazis were gone, but there were plenty of villains:

on the left the Commies, on the right the McCarthyites.
Poor Dale, you had a horse, too, what was her name? You were

Queen of the West until you gained a hundred pounds on fried
rashers, doughnuts, Wonder Bread, and bakery cakes. Okay,

so it couldn't last forever. Get over it, Trigger, I tell myself,
television is fickle. Now it's hospital shows, blood and angst

undercut with tawdry sex. I blame the French, frigging cinema
verité. Where's the story, the hero, the beautiful girl?

Where's the horse? The other dead horses say, Whoa, don't get
excited, Trigger. Nothing's the way it was. That's the truth. Ah,

youth, I try not to be bitter, but sometimes I dream about
Zorro, now there was a guy who could make a horse look good.

Ode on My Wasted Youth

Is there anything so ridiculous as being twenty
       and carrying around a copy of *Being and Nothingness*,
so boys will think you have a fine mind
       when really your brain is a whirling miasma,
a rat's nest erected by Jehovah, Rousseau, Dante,
       George Eliot, and Bozo the Clown?
I might as well have been in costume and on stage,
       I was so silly, but with no appreciation
of my predicament, like a dim-bulb ingenue
       with a fluffy wig being bamboozled by a cad
whose insincerity oozes from every orifice,
       but she thinks he's spiritual, only I was playing
both roles, hoodwinking myself with ideas
       that couldn't and wouldn't do me much good, buying berets,
dreaming of Paris and utter degradation,
       like Anaïs Nin under Henry Miller or vice versa.
Other people were getting married and buying cars,
       but not me, and I wasn't even looking for Truth,
just some kind of minor grip on the whole enchilada,
       and I could see why so many went for eastern cults,
because of all religions Hinduism is the only one
       that seems to recognize the universal mess
and attack it with a set of ideas even wackier
       than said cosmos, and I think of all
my mistaken notions, like believing "firmament"
       meant "earth" and then finding out it meant "sky,"
which is not firm at all, though come to find out the substance
       under our feet is rather lacking in solidity as well.
Oh, words, my very dear friends,
       whether in single perfection—mordant, mellifluous,

multilingual—or crammed together

     in a gold-foil-wrapped chocolate valentine

like *Middlemarch*, how could I have survived without you,

     the bread, the meat, the absolute confection,

like the oracles at Delphi drinking their mad honey,

     opening my box of darkness with your tiny, insistent flame.

Ode to Untoward Dreams

Have you ever dreamt you had sex with someone
        you aren't remotely interested in,
like a guy you work with or one of your husband's friends,
        and then the next time you see him,
at the Xerox machine or a party,
        you're horribly embarrassed
and the poor guy has no idea what's going on
        and neither do you,
because you hardly ever see your husband's friend,
        since his wife can't stand you
because you are childless, thus selfish,
        and your conversation is filled
with utter drivel, like the sex lives of movie stars
        and all your various fears and phobias,
which since she's a psychologist she should find
        at least remotely interesting,
but guess what, she doesn't,
        and she doesn't even know what you and her husband
are doing at night, and the guy at work,
        who could have guessed that he would do
those kind of things and with such abandon,
        it makes you wonder about his mousey wife
and what's going on there, if anything.
        Freud said all dreams are wish fulfillments,
but sometimes it's hard to figure out the exact meaning
        of your desire, though in the case
of your husband's friend,
        maybe you identify with his wife
because in some ways you hate yourself
        as much as she seems to,

though for completely different reasons,
       and the guy at work,
who knows, it was probably the garlic tart
       you had for dinner or the four beers,
and maybe you are drinking too much these days,
       though it rarely seems like enough,
your spine crawling up your back,
       like a rat in a Skinner box, shaking so hard
at times you think you either have epilepsy
       or are on the verge of samadhi,
though neither is your dream come true:
       nirvana seems boring
and epilepsy, well, who needs more problems,
       because when we close our eyes each night,
it's review time, *quel calvaire*,
       familiar but hideous,
despite the sexual release with odd partners,
       and running down a tawdry neon street
you find yourself aloft, soaring
       over the paltry world, so far away
it suddenly seems lovely,
       like an intricate toy town,
with tiny perfect people doing tiny perfect things,
       but you always plummet to earth, a hard fall
into the amorous arms of the most peculiar people,
       yet everyone has his attractions,
so when your husband tries to wake you,
       you say, wait, wait, one more fall, one more kiss.

Ode to the Lost Luggage Warehouse at the Rome Airport

Until you've visited the lost luggage warehouse
        at the Rome airport in August, you have not lived,
the Mediterranean sun insinuating itself
        into the inner sucking marrow of your bones,
roasting your epidermis like a holiday bird's,
        a goose, upon reflection, would be the fitting
analogy. You hear the faint sizzling of the fat
        under your skin, organs grilling, brain singed
as you walk to the guardhouse and show the uniformed
        sentinel your paper that certifies you have indeed
lost your bag. You gaze at his amazing hat with plumes
        tinted maroon and gold while he scrutinizes your clutch

of ragged forms, signed by Signor Nardo Ferrari,
        minor functionary with the state airline
at the *ufficio* in Firenze, who has confided
        in beautiful English he will retire at the end
of the month and devote himself to the cultivation
        of vegetables and fruit, a noble endeavor,
but you suspect he'll not be leaving his lush *paradiso*
        to iron out your petty problems. You have come in pursuit
of your bag, supplicant on a holy quest to retrieve
        that which is your own, or was once your own,
the dresses, coat, boots, and intimate et cetera,
        nothing priceless, no treasures as such, but dear to you,

especially the black coat you bought in Paris
        in a decrepit building below Sacre Coeur,
going with Marie after lunch, giving the secret password,
        hearing the answering hiss, walking up four flights

of stairs to a room filled with ugly clothes,
　　　　　one divine coat, now lost in the dark regions
of this Italian underworld, you hope, for if not here,
　　　　　it's apparently nowhere. This warehouse is a warren
of high-ceilinged rooms with thousands of bags stacked
　　　　　on metal shelves, precariously piled backpacks
with scurf from Katmandu, Malmö, Khartoum, Köln, Kraków,
　　　　　Istanbul, Reims in France or Francia in *italiano*,

chic makeup cases, black bags like the suitcases of doom,
　　　　　hard-shelled portmanteaus like turtles (soft parts
incognito, mating in tandem), briefcases, carpet bags,
　　　　　19th-century trunks with straps and buckles,
and you see a woman, *molto doloroso*, in latex gloves,
　　　　　a surgeon delving, methodically, in a suitcase
filled with Japanese snacks—arare, dried squid, rice candy
　　　　　wrapped in thin edible paper, red and green jellied sweets—
recognized from your childhood in Hawai'i, and amid
　　　　　the *conglomerazione* of heat, memory, and rage you imagine
a Japanese man, thinking, I'm going to Italy, but the food,
　　　　　I'll hate it. Then packing all his favorites: the sublime

shredded mango of blessed memory, cracked plum, dried peas,
　　　　　and you think of Sei Shonagun, supercilious court lady
in 10th century Japan because you are reading her Pillow Book,
　　　　　a record of things that disgust or please her,
and you whip your kimono around and say,
　　　　　"Things I adore about Rome: the lingerie stores
for nuns with their fifties bulletproof brassieres
　　　　　and other medieval undies, the floor of St. Peter's

with its measurements of the lesser cathedrals

      of the world (Milan, Florence, St. Paul's in London),

Caravaggio's *St. Paul* and *Virgin of Loreto.*

      Things that disgust me in August: backpacks with cheese,

child carriers imbedded with the scum of mashed

      bananas and cereal, petroleum laced breezes

from jet exhaust, the color navy blue." Your Italian

      is meager but the denizens of this particular realm

of hell are courteous if lethargic and show you

      that the bags are stacked by month:

agosto, luglio, giugno, but that's as far

      as they go. No Joe DiMaggio or before. To be

anywhere else is all you want. You hate your clothes,

      no coat's worth the flames licking your feet.

You take a careful waltz through the months,

      and find nothing in the midst of so much.

The whole long way back to Florence, while the gorgeous

      panorama of the countryside flies by,

you have a *caffè,* try to read, but a few seats down

      a child screams, hysterical with fatigue,

and you see his face with its sticky impasto of snot,

      candy and tears, and you think of all your losses,

those past and the ones to come, your own death,

      il tuo morto, which makes the loss of a French coat,

shoes, and a few dresses seem ridiculous.

      You think of your arrival in Florence, the walk home

from the station past the Duomo, your husband's hands,

      his kisses and the dinner you'll eat, prosciutto

and melone, perhaps some ravioli in a restaurant
        near the Sant'Ambrogio market, you'll buy a new coat
for winter, an Italian coat, *il soprabito*,
        one more beautiful than the one lost. That's the way
your life will go, one day after another,
        until you begin your kamikaze run toward death.
It makes you sick to think of it until you begin
        to get used to the idea. I'd better get busy,
you think, enjoy life, be good to others,
        drink more wine, fill a suitcase with arare,
dried squid. When you leave home anything can happen.
        You may be caught in a foreign country one day,

without money, clothes or anything good to eat,
        and you'll have to try those stinky chitterlings,
brine-soaked pig knuckles, poached brains quivering
        on a wooden platter, tripe, baked ear wax,
fried grasshoppers, ant cakes, dirt souffles,
        and though it seems impossible, they could prove
delicious or at the very least nourishing.
        Don't make a fool of yourself, and one day
you may join Signor Ferrari in his bosky Eden.
        Everyone will be there God, Jesus and Mary,
your mother and father, even your pain-in-the-ass sister
        who got everything. Heaven, you hate it:

the conversation's boring, and everyone's so sane,
        so well-adjusted. And it's cold. Heaven should be warm,
a bit like Hawai'i, so you're upset, and then you see
        your sister, and she's not cold because she's wearing

your French coat. But you're not in heaven, you're on a train,
    going faster, it seems, as you approach Florence.
You're in a muddle, glum, have nothing to show
    for your day but a headache and a blister
on your heel. You want the train to crash,
    blow you to kingdom come. You want your mother
to kiss you, call you Baby, Darling; you'd sell
    your soul for some shredded mango or dried plum.

BABEL

(2004)

My Translation

I am translating the world into mockingbird, into blue jay,
  into cat-bombing avian obbligato, because I want
more noise, more bells, more senseless tintinnabulation,
  more crow, thunder, squawk, more bird song,
more Beethoven, more philharmonic mash notes to the gods.
  I am translating the world into onyx, into Abyssinian,
into pale blue Visigoth vernacular, because the bloody earth
  is not one color, one stripe, one smooth mulatto
café con leche cream-colored dream, no rumba, no cha-cha,
  no cheek-to-cheek tango through the Argentine
midnight stream, but a hodgepodge of rival factions
  fighting over the borders of nothing. I am translating
the world into blue, azure, cerulean, because there is a sky
  beneath us as there is a sea above. O the fish soar
like dragonflies through empyrean clouds; the mockingbird
  swims through the ocean like a man-of-war. I am
translating the heavens into Gutenberg, into Bodoni,
  into offset digital karmic Palatino, every "T" a crucifix
on the shrine of my lexicographic longing. I am reading
  the archaic language of birches, frangipani pidgin of monsoon,
Bali palm dialect of endless summer. I am translating the sky
  into bulls, swans, gold dust, for a god is filled with such power
that mortal husbands quiver in the shadow of his furious lust,
  the bliss-driven engine of his thrumming mythopoesis.
I am calling the world to take off its veils of fog and soot,
  shed its overcoat of factories, highways, skyscrapers,
lay down its rocks, roots, rivers, and lie naked in my naked arms,
  for I am translating the earth and all its dominions
into desire, into flayed skin screaming abandon, all tongue,
  mouth, flesh-drunk erotic demonology, fiery seraphim

mating with mortals, wings incinerated in the white heat
        of love, Apollo turning Daphne into marble, into tree roots,
into chlorophyll, scent of cut grass, a baby's mouth sweet
        with milk, because this is my Cultural Revolution,
my Mao Tse Tung, my Chou En-Lai, my attempt to go
        without sin, to have it my way no matter what, for I am
the way, the truth, the light, third empress of the seventh dynasty,
        Madame Chiang, Madame Nhu, Madame X, Madame
Three Quarters of the Left Brain, poster girl of a million GIs,
        Betty Grable to you, buster, Jane Russell, all gams, breasts,
blond smiles, brunette tribulation, Betty and Veronica,
        the last stop before Kiss-and-Tell, Texas, Fourth
Shepherdess of confabulation, Calliope's stepdaughter, Erato's
        girl, it's all Greek to me, for I am translating the world
as if it were a bomb, a thief, a book. Chapter One: the noun
        of my mother's womb, verb of birth, adjectives of blood,
screams, fluorescence. Chapter Two: explosions of words
        growing into sentences, arms, legs, tentacles. Chapter Three:
voyages to unheard-of territories—here be monsters, two-mile
        waterfalls, portals to the underworld. Chapter Four: returns,
for in all of us there's an Odysseus ready to misunderstand the sky
        and its garbled signs, rumble-thunder theater of missed cues,
because this is our adventure, our calling, our do-or-die
        mission, translating the world into the body's bright lie.

The Mockingbird on the Buddha

The mockingbird on the Buddha says, Where's my seed,
          you Jezebel, where's the sunshine in my blue sky,
where's the Hittite princess, Pharaoh's temple, where's the rain
          for the misery I love so much? The mockingbird
on the Buddha scolds the tree for trying to stay straight
          in the hurricane of words blowing out of the cold north,
wind like screams, night like brandy on the dark cut of my heart.
          The mockingbird on the Buddha, music is his life,
he hears the tunes of the universe, cacophony of calypso,
          hacking cough in the black lung of desire; he's ruddy
with lust, that sweet stepping puffed-up old gray bird o' mine.
          The mockingbird on the Buddha says, Eat up
while the night is young. Have some peach cobbler, girl,
          have some fried oysters, have some Pouligny
Montrachet, *ma chère*, for the night is coming, and you need meat
          on your bones to ride that wild horse. The mockingbird
on the Buddha says, It's time for a change, little missy. You've
          been in charge too long. It's time for the bird
to take over, because he stays up late, knows what night can be,
          past twelve, past two, when trouble's dark and beautiful.
You never knew what hit you, and that's the best feeling
          in the whole wide world. The mockingbird
on the Buddha makes his nest inside my brain: he looks good
          in gray, gets fat on thought, he's my enemy,
my Einstein, my ever-loving monkey boy, every monkey thought
          I blame on him, every night so sweet my body breaks
apart like a Spanish galleon raining gold on the ocean floor.

Idolatry

My Baal, shimmering Apollo, junkyard Buonarroti,
        funkadelic *malocchio*, voice shouting
from the radio, talking about love, about heartbreak,
        about doing everything you can till you can't do
no more. Then you float by in a Coupe de Ville,
        hair conked, wearing the mink stole
of delicious indifference, reciting the odes
        of Mr. John Keats like you was his best friend.
I was minding my own business, being good as a girl
        can be when every inch of skin aches
for the sky. Where is my wide sky, now all I see
        is you? Where is my ocean, you hex on thought,
golden calf in the living room of ambition, pagan call,
        demon whispering like beetles on the skin
of morning. I hear your voice come out of the mouths
        of little girls jumping rope on Orange Avenue.
I hear your aria in the shopping center pharmacy,
        in the tired lines around the eyes
of every sleepless night. You're an astronomer,
        roaming the heavens, a flyboy anatomist,
dissecting the stars. Tell me again about the stars,
        those cheap flashcards of the gods. Tell me
about human sacrifice, the huju rituals of versification,
        the quantum mechanics of line, my holy-of-holies,
sanctum sanctorum, my hideaway in the world of cool.
        Pagan huckster, heat up your spells, your charms,
your rapture, I come to you a novice, an acolyte,
        a scullery maid in the choir of the unruly. Give me
my music, my words, my lyrical demonstration
        of all that is gorgeous and invisible. I am

your handmaiden, your courtesan, your ten-cents-a-dance
        barroom floozie. My Lord-who-whispers-his-secrets-
into-the-skulls-of-angels, your slightest whim is my delight.
        Every day I wake to your disciples' quick trill.
I am the prisoner of your darkest sigh, queen of ungovernable
        birds. You visit me at night when the sky is a veil
of stars, but your shame is an aphrodisiac, a love potion,
        a quick fix in the alley from the dark drug of words.

O Deceitful Tongue

> You love all words that devour, O deceitful tongue.
>
> —Psalms 52:4

Rogue slab in the slaughterhouse of the mouth,
you love all words that whistle like bombs

through the delphinium sky. O tongue that sucks
honey from the vinegar bush—demagogue, street

preacher, cutpurse at the afternoon hanging—break
my neck a thousand times till I remember the digits

of your prime number. Drunk tongue, warling,
malt-mad forger in the bone orchard, give me

your traitor's code, so I can whistle my psalm
through the sinworm night. Tongue of rough

bread, blues tongue, wolf tongue. Kiss me,
deceitful mouth, smash my curtain of skin, devour

the air wild with bees, swallow their wings,
make me a bloody hive for their bitter queen.

Vex Me

Vex me, O Night, your stars stuttering like a stuck jukebox,
put a spell on me, my bones atremble at your tabernacle

of rhythm and blues. Call out your archers, chain me
to a wall, let the stone fortress of my body fall

like a rabid fox before an army of dogs. Rebuke me,
rip out my larynx like a lazy snake and feed it to the voiceless

throng. For I am midnight's girl, scouring unlit streets
like Persephone stalking her swarthy lord. Anoint me

with oil, make me greasy as a fast-food fry. Deliver me
like a pizza to the snapping crack-house hours between

one and four. Build me an ark, fill it with prairie moths,
split-winged fritillaries, blue-bottle flies. Stitch

me a gown of taffeta and quinine, starlight and nightsoil,
and when the clock tocks two, I'll be the belle of the malaria ball.

Fang

I want to be seven feet tall, walk out of the Gabon bush,
  speaking Fang, to gaze into the sky and see
    an overturned bowl of godless blue, a wild storm
  in the heart of the devil, a rocky sea of scudding,
    poisoned boats. I want to look into the dark canopy
  of trees and hear the mother of all talking creatures,
fluttering mountains, a green sea swimming with fish that fly.
  I need Fang for revenge—fire smoldering
    in the heart, a quick knife, a sickness
that fells grown men in the midday sun. I want words
  like teeth that could tear the flesh
    from the throat of my worst enemy—her face
  staring at me from every mirror. Every morning
my voice is a bird flying over treetops,
    dropping berries bitter and sweet
  into mouths open and closed. I can hardly bear
the sun on my skin. O Fang, come to me as a suitor
  with two goats and an orchard of pomegranates, woo me
    with your straight back, take me deep
into the night when stars fall like faithless lovers
  on the black trees. I need the mouth of a viper,
    a vampire, a mad dog pulling children
  from their mothers' arms. I want my heart to swell
like a wide brown river carrying trees, huts, limbs
    to the flood-maddened sea. O Fang,
  heart of a snake, body of impenetrable water,
    dark continent of betel nut and monkeypod,
erupt from my tongue, give me a world I cannot give myself.

Thus Spake the Mockingbird

The mockingbird says, hallelujah, coreopsis, I make the day
       bright, I wake the night-blooming jasmine. I am
the duodecimo of desperate love, the hocus-pocus passion
       flower of delirious retribution. You never saw such a bird,
such a triage of blood and feathers, tongue and bone. O the world
       is a sad address, bitterness melting the tongues of babies,
breasts full of accidental milk, but I can teach the flowers to grow,
       take their tight buds, unfurl them like flags in the morning heat,
fat banners of scent, flat platters of riot on the emerald scene.
       I am the green god of pine trees, conducting the music
of rustling needles through a harp of wind. I am the heart of men,
       the wild bird that drives their sex, forges their engines,
jimmies their shattered locks in the dark flare where midnight slinks.
       I am the careless minx in the skirts of women, the bright moon
caressing their hair, the sharp words pouring from their beautiful mouths
       in board rooms, on bar stools, in big city launderettes. I am
Lester Young's sidewinding sax, sending that Pony Express
       message out west in the Marconi tube hidden in every torso
tied tight in the corset of do and don't, high and low, yes and no. I am
       the radio, first god of the twentieth century, broadcasting
the news, the blues, the death counts, the mothers wailing
       when everyone's gone home. I am sweeping
through the Eustachian tubes of the great plains, transmitting
       through every ear of corn, shimmying down the spine
of every Bible-thumping banker and bureaucrat, relaying the anointed
       word of the shimmering world. Every dirty foot that walks
the broken streets moves on my wings. I speak from the golden
       screens. Hear the roar of my discord murdering the trees,
screaming its furious rag, the fuselage of my revival-tent brag. Open
       your windows, slip on your castanets. I am the flamenco
in the heel of desire. I am the dancer. I am the choir. Hear my wild
       throat crowd the exploding sky. O I can make a noise.

Ode to American English

I was missing English one day, American, really,

      with its pill-popping Hungarian goulash of everything

from Anglo-Saxon to Zulu, because British English

      is not the same, if the paperback dictionary

I bought at Brentano's on the Avenue de l'Opéra

      is any indication, too cultured by half. Oh, the English

know their delphiniums, but what about doowop, donuts,

      Dick Tracy, Tricky Dick? With their elegant Oxfordian

accents, how could they understand my yearning for the hotrod,

      hotdog, hot flash vocabulary of the U. S. of A.,

the fragmented fandango of Dagwood's everyday flattening

      of Mr. Beasley on the sidewalk, fetuses floating

on billboards, drive-by monster hip-hop stereos shaking

      the windows of my dining room like a 7.5 earthquake,

Ebonics, Spanglish, "you know" used as comma and period,

      the inability of 90% of the population to get the present perfect:

I have went, I have saw, I have tooken Jesus into my heart,

      the battle cry of the Bible Belt, but no one uses

the King James anymore, only plain-speak versions,

      in which Jesus, raising Lazarus from the dead, says,

"Dude, wake up," and the L-man bolts up like a B-movie

      mummy. "Whoa, I was toasted." Yes, ma'am,

I miss the mongrel plenitude of American English, its fall-guy,

      rat-terrier, dog-pound neologisms, the bomb of it all,

the rushing River Jordan backwoods mutability of it, the low-rider,

      boom-box cruise of it, from New Joisey to Ha-wah-ya

with its sly dog, malasada-scarfing beach blanket lingo

      to the ubiquitous Valley Girl's *like-like* stuttering,

shopaholic rant. I miss its quotidian beauty, its querulous

      back-biting righteous indignation, its preening rotgut

flag-waving cowardice. *Suffering Succotash*, sputters

        Sylvester the Cat; *sine die*, say the pork-bellied legislators

of the swamps and plains. I miss all those guys, their Tweety-bird

        resilience, their Doris Day optimism, the candid unguent

of utter unhappiness on every channel, the midnight televangelist

        euphoric stew, the junk mail, voice mail vernacular.

On every *boulevard* and *rue* I miss the Tarzan cry of Johnny

        Weismueller, Johnny Cash, Johnny B. Goode,

and all the smart-talking, gum-snapping hard-girl dialogue,

        finger-popping x-rated street talk, sports babble,

Cheetoes, Cheerios, chili dog diatribes. Yeah, I miss them all,

        sitting here on my sidewalk throne sipping champagne

verses lined up like hearses, metaphors juking, nouns zipping

        in my head like Corvettes on Dexedrine, French verbs

slitting my throat, yearning for James Dean to jump my curb.

Ode to Hardware Stores

Where have all the hardware stores gone—dusty, sixty-watt
        warrens with wood floors, cracked linoleum,
poured concrete painted blood red? Where are Eppes, Terry Rosa,
        Yon's, Flint—low buildings on South Monroe,
Eighth Avenue, Gaines Street with their scent of paint thinner,
        pesticides, plastic hoses coiled like serpents
in a garden paradisal with screws in buckets or bins
        against a brick wall with hand-lettered signs
in ball-point pen—*Carriage screws, two dozen for fifty cents*—
        long vicious dry-wall screws, thick wood screws
like peasants digging potatoes in fields, thin elegant trim
        screws—New York dames at a backwoods hick
Sunday School picnic. O universal clevis pins, seven holes
        in the shank, like the seven deadly sins.
Where are the men—Mr. Franks, Mr. Piggot, Tyrone, Hank,
        Ralph—sunburnt with stomachs and no asses,
men who knew the mythology of nails, Zeuses enthroned
        on an Olympus of weak coffee, bad haircuts,
and tin cans of galvanized casing nails, sinker nails, brads,
        20-penny common nails, duplex head nails, flooring nails
like railroad spikes, finish nails, fence staples, cotter pins,
        roofing nails—flat-headed as Floyd Crawford,
who lived next door to you for years but would never say hi
        or make eye contact. What a career in hardware
he could have had, his blue-black hair slicked back with brilliantine,
        rolling a toothpick between his teeth while sorting
screw eyes and carpet tacks. Where are the hardware stores,
        open Monday through Friday, Saturday till two?
No night hours here, like physicists their universe mathematical
        and pure in its way: dinner at six, *Rawhide* at eight,

lights out at ten, kiss in the dark, up at five for the subatomic world
       of toggle bolts, cap screws, hinch-pin clips, split-lock
washers. And the tools—saws, rakes, wrenches, ratchets, drills,
       chisels, and hose heads, hose couplings, sandpaper
(garnet, production, wet or dry), hinges, wire nails, caulk, nuts,
       lag screws, pulleys, vise grips, hexbolts, fender washers,
all in a primordial stew of laconic talk about football, baseball,
       who'll start for the Dodgers, St. Louis, the Phillies,
the Cubs? Walk around the block today and see their ghosts:
       abandoned lots, graffitti'd windows, and tacked
to backroom walls, pin-up calendars almost decorous
       in our porn-riddled galaxy of Walmarts, Seven-Elevens,
stripmalls like strip mines or a carrion bird's curved beak
       gobbling farms, meadows, wildflowers, drowsy afternoons
of nothing to do but watch dust motes dance through a streak
       of sunlight in a darkened room. If there's a second coming,
I want angels called Lem, Nelson, Rodney, and Cletis gathered
       around a bin of nails, their silence like hosannahs,
hallelujahs, amens swelling from cinderblock cathedrals
       drowning our cries of *bigger, faster, more, more, more.*

Ode to Barbecue

We are lost again in the middle of redneck nowhere,
        which is a hundred times scarier
than any other nowhere because everyone has guns.
        Let me emphasize that plural—rifles,
double-barreled shotguns, .22 semiautomatics,
        12-gauge pumps, .357 magnums. And for what?
Barbecue. A friend of a friend's student's cousin's
        aunt's husband was a cook in the army
for 30 years, and he has retired to rural Georgia
        with the sole aim in his artistic soul of creating
the best barbecued ribs in the universe and, according
        to rumor, he has succeeded, which is not surprising
because this is a part of the world where the artistic soul
        rises up like a phoenix from the pit of rattlesnake
churches and born-again retribution, where Charlie Lucas
        the Tin Man creates dinosaurs, colossi of rusted
steel bands and garbage can mamas with radiator torsos,
        electric-coil hearts, fingers of screws. Here W. C. Rice's
Cross Garden grows out of the southern red clay with rusted
        Buicks shouting, "The Devil Will Put Your Soul
in Hell Burn It Forever" and "No Water in Hell," and I think
        of Chet Baker singing "Let's Get Lost," and I know
what he means, because more and more I know
        where I am, and I don't like the feeling,
and Chet knew about Hell and maybe about being saved,
        something much talked about in the Deep South,
being saved and being lost because we are all sinners,
        amen, we bear Adam's stain, and the only way
to heaven is to be washed in the blood of the Lamb,
        which is kind of what happens when out of the South

Georgia woods we see a little shack with smoke

pouring from the chimney though it's August

and steamier than a mild day in Hell; we sit at a picnic table

and a broad-bellied man sets down plates of ribs,

a small mountain of red meat, so different from Paris

where for my birthday my husband took me

to an elegant place where we ate tiny ribs washed down

with a sublime St.-Josèphe. Oh, don't get me wrong,

they were good, but the whole time I was out of sorts,

squirming on my perfect chair, disgruntled,

because I wanted to be at Tiny Register's, Kojack's,

J. B.'s, I wanted ribs all right but big juicy ribs dripping

with sauce, the secret recipe handed down from grandmother

to father to son, sauce that could take the paint off a Buick,

a hot, sin-lacerating concoction of tomatoes, jalapeños

and sugar, washed down with iced tea, Coca-Cola, beer,

because there's no water in Hell, and Hell is hot, oh yeah.

Ode on Satan's Power

At a local bistro's Christmas sing-along, the new
　　　age pianist leads us in a pan-cultural brew
of seasonal songs, the Ramadan chant being my
　　　personal favorite, though the Kwanza lullaby
and Hanukkah round are *very interesting.* Let's
　　　face it, most of us are there for the carols we set
to memory in childhood though some lyrics have been
　　　changed, so when we sing "God Rest Ye Merry, Gentlemen,"
we're transformed into a roomful of slightly tipsy
　　　middle-class *gentlepeople* who are longing to be
saved from *hopelessness* instead of *Satan's power when*
　　　we were gone astray, but I, for one, sing out *Satan's*
power as do most of the *gentlepeople,* women

and men, something I find myself pondering a few
　　　days later, while my profoundly worried nephew,
Henry, and I embark on our annual blitzkrieg
　　　of baking, punctuated by Henry's high speed
philosophical questioning, such as, Where do we
　　　go when we die? Pressing my collection of cookie
cutters—trees, snowflakes, Santas—into fragrant ginger
　　　dough, I want to say, *Who cares? Carpe diem, buster,*
though, of course, I'm way too scarred by pop psychology
　　　to utter half the nutty things that pop up like weeds
in the 18th-century garden of my brain. Eight-
　　　year-olds need their questions answered, I suppose, but not
by me. "Let's watch some TV," I say, an instrument

of Satan if ever there was one. *Bullitt's* on—Steve
　　　McQueen in his prime. I love this movie—equal waves

of sorrow and carnage washed up on a hokey late-

        sixties beach of masculine cool. McQueen is Bullitt,
and Jacqueline Bisset's his girl. Henry and I start

        watching during the scene where she is driving Bullitt
around because, if I remember correctly, he's

        totaled not just one but several cars, in at least
as many now-famous chases. Jackie drops Bullitt

        at a hotel, where he finds a girl, newly dead, throat
circled with purple fingerprints like grape jam stains. "What

        happened to her?" Henry asks, frowning. I think, *Oh, shit,
this is not an officially approved nephew-aunt*

Christmas activity. If I don't make a big deal

        of it, maybe he won't tell his mother. "Someone strangled
her," I say. "What's strangled?" he asks, and I see my sister

        has chosen not to threaten her child as our own dear
mother routinely threatened us. Driven crazy, she

        browbeat us with strangulation, being slapped silly,
public humiliation, murder, and eternal

        damnation. Perhaps because Henry's her only child,
my sister can afford to be gentler with her son,

        or maybe it's because two months before he was born
she almost lost him, ending up in the hospital,

        hooked to machines, ordered to bed for the final
wrenching weeks. Maybe that's why the story of the Christ child

speaks to us. All parents wonder how the world will treat

        their tender babes. Like Lorca, will he become a great
poet, then end up in a mass grave? Only German

        philosophers think more about death than Henry Gwynn.

"Why did he strangle her?" he asks, face formidable
        as Hegel's. *Satan's power*, I want to scream, but mumble
"It's just a movie; it's not real." Steve McQueen's dodging
        a plane, and I remember reading he did his own
stunts, which I tell Henry, but he's still in that hotel
        room. "If she was alive, how'd she get her eyes to roll
back into her head?" I'm thinking of pornography,
        snuff movies, all the things I never want him to see
or even know about in this tawdry world. "Honey,

it's a major motion picture. Even in a small part
        an actress has to be great." He nods and takes a bite
off Santa's head. "She was a pretty good actress." You
        bet your booty, and I realize out of the blue
Santa is an anagram for Satan. No way am
        I going to explain anagrams or Herr Satan,
though how wonderful to have such a nemesis—
        a fallen archangel, one of high heaven's brightest stars—
in a battle with Jehovah for our souls, rather
        than the calendar's increasing speed like a roller
coaster run amok through a fun park of lost dreams, lost
        landscapes, and children, growing up faster than we thought
possible in the last terrible days before their birth.

Ode to My 1977 Toyota

Engine like a Singer sewing machine, where have you
      not carried me—to dance class, grocery shopping,
into the heart of darkness and back again? O the fruit
      you've transported—cherries, peaches, blueberries,
watermelons, thousands of Fuji apples—books,
      and all my dark thoughts, the giddy ones, too,
like bottles of champagne popped at the wedding of two people
      who will pass each other on the street as strangers
in twenty years. Ronald Reagan was president when I walked
      into Big Chief Motors and saw you glimmering
on the lot like a slice of broiled mahi mahi or sushi
      without its topknot of tuna. Remember the months
I drove you to work singing "Some Enchanted Evening?"
      Those were scary times. All I thought about
was getting on I-10 with you and not stopping. Would you
      have made it to New Orleans? What would our life
have been like there? I'd forgotten about poetry. Thank God,
      I remembered her. She saved us both. We were young
together. Now we're not. College boys stop us at traffic lights
      and tell me how cool you are. Like an ice cube, I say,
though you've never had air conditioning. Who needed it?
      I would have missed so many smells without you—
confederate jasmine, magnolia blossoms, the briny sigh
      of the Gulf of Mexico, rotting 'possums scattered
along 319 between Sopchoppy and Panacea. How many holes
      are there in the ballet shoes in your back seat?
How did that pair of men's white loafers end up in your trunk?
      Why do I have so many questions, and why
are the answers like the animals that dart in front of your headlights
      as we drive home from the coast, the Milky Way

strung across the black velvet bowl of the sky like the tiara
        of some impossibly fat empress who rules the universe
but doesn't know if tomorrow is December or Tuesday or June first.

Ode on My Mother's Handwriting

Her *a*'s are like small rolls warm from the oven, yeasty,
          fragrant, one identical to the other, molded
by a master baker, serious about her craft, but comical, too,
          smudge of flour on her sharp nose, laughing
with her workers, urging them to eat, eat, eat, but demanding
          the most gorgeous cakes in Christendom.
Her *b*'s are upright as soldiers trained by harsh sergeants,
          whose invective seems cruel in the bower of one's
own country but becomes hot gruel and a wool coat
          during January on the steppes outside Moscow.
Would that every infant could nestle in the warm crook
          of her *c*'s, taste the sweet milk of her *d*'s, hear
the satiny coos of her nonsense whisperings, making
          the three-pronged razor of her *E* easier to take,
the *bad girl, I'm ashamed of you, disappointed, hateful,*
          shame, shame, shame, the blistering fury
of her *f* feel less like the sharpened rapier of a paid assassin,
          left only with the desire to be good, to be ushered
again into the glittering palace of her good graces,
          for her *g*'s are great and fail not, their mercy
is everlasting. The house of her *h* is a plain building. It has no
          pediments or Palladian windows but brick walls,
sturdy and indestructible. Oh, the mighty storms that rage
          cannot tear down these thick walls or alter
their sturdy heart. But her windows are small—she does not
          like to look out, shuts her eyes, for the world
is cold while her fire is warm. She is a household god,
          jumped up on Jesus, Jeremiah, Job, all the Old
Testament scallywags and their raving pomaded televangelist
          progeny, yet her *k*'s know how to kick up their heels,

laugh at you and with you, whip up a Christmas Dickens
   would envy, kiss your eyelids as you drift off to sleep,
though no one can know the loneliness of her *l*, a forlorn
   obelisk in the desert, hard and bitterly cold
in the heat of the sun. Other *m*'s are soft and round,
   but not hers—the answer to every supplication
is, "N-O spells no," which, in a way, is comforting,
   because you know where you stand,
where your please, *pretty please* begins, and how far those *p*'s
   must climb before meeting her most serene
and imperial *q*'s—regular, rigid, redoubtable. For the dark wind
   of her *s*'s can be like the desert simoom, hot and dry.
You could die of thirst, your throat taut as a tent pole holding up
   your bones and their tatters of flesh, but for her hurricane
of words, blowing roofs off houses, lavishing water on an arid world,
   unleashing slaps, hugs, prayers on the long, ungainly hours
that separate us like the spaces between her lines, the waves
   of her *u*'s, slice of her *v*'s, vivisecting each moment
with the x-ray of her ecclesiastical gaze. What is her *x*, a kiss
   or a rebuke? Both—her lips sweet as the nectar
bees suck from flowers, cruel as their sting. So why
   am I still her acolyte, her disciple, her most obstreperous
slave? Because in the curve of her *zed* is my Zen master,
   my beginning and my end. How I have felt the five
fingers of her one hand; seen her hair, once chestnut, turn white
   as a seraph's wings; heard her high, naked voice combust
with love's bitter perfume; sat down at her Puritan
   table and feasted on her wild blue eyes, like rustling
cornflowers in the dark, mutinous grass of the past.

ALL-NIGHT LINGO TANGO

(2009)

Ode to Anglo Saxon, Film Noir, and the Hundred Thousand Anxieties That Plague Me Like Demons in a Medieval Christian Allegory

Yo, Viking dudes, who knew your big-dog cock-of-the-walk
        raping and pillaging would put us all here, right smack
dab in the middle of a decade filled with the stink
        of war? Yes, sir, boys and girls, we're eating an old sock
sandwich, but we're speaking English, kind of a weird fluke
        (a piece of luck, not the parasite), because the kick-
ass Angles were illiterate hicks while the sublime Greeks
        had been writing poetry for a thousand years, heck,
history and philosophy, too, though they did shellac
        the Trojans and a lot of other guys as well, stuck
them with their Bronze Age swords, testosterone run amok,
        or so I'm thinking here from my present perch—a swank
appartement à Paris, swilling champagne, clothes black,
        as if my past were *un chef d'oeuvre* by Jan van Eyck,
the soundtrack written by Johann Sebastian Bach
        or his son, rather than the Three Stooges-Lawrence Welk
debacle that really occurred. My mind's a train wreck
        of two lingoes, twenty-six letters, and thousands of quick
images from movies, French—yes, but mostly *aw-shucks-
        ma'am* Hollywood Westerns or *policiers* in stark
black and white, and I'm the twist, tomato, skirt, the weak
        sister who rats out her grifter boyfriend, palms a deck
of Luckies she puffs while scheming with the private dick
        to pocket twenty large, or I'm the classy dame, sick
of her stinking rich life and her Ralph Bellamy schmuck
        of a boyfriend. That's when Bogart's three-pack-a-day croak
(dialogue by Raymond Chandler) sounds like music,
        maybe John Coltrane, and you're up the five-and-dime creek,

ma chère, because love can turn you into a mark, punk,

  jingle-brained two-bit patsy who'd take a fast sawbuck
for snitching out her squeeze to the cops. Or you're the crack

  whore with an MBA standing on the corner in chic
Versace rags, falling for the DA till the Czech

  drug lord plugs him. So who are you? Not the hippie chick
of your early twenties or the Sears and Roebuck

  Christian drudge your mother became, though Satan still stalks
you on a regular basis. Is that guy a slick

  operator or what with his Brylcreemed hair and pock-
marked face? There's still smallpox in Hell, so you push him back

  whenever you can, grow orchids and for dinner cook
risotto alla Milanese, because *knick, knack*

  paddy whack, you're counting on something, not luck or rock
and roll, though you've been there—at the HIC with Mick

  Jagger prancing around like a hopped-up jumping jack
on speed. No, *ma petite* Marcella Proust, this is the joke:

  when your mother prays for you, your stuttering heart ticks
a little more like a Swiss-made watch, and when you speak,

  does French come out? Nah, it's the echo of those shock-jock
Vikings, hacking their way across Europe, red-haired, drunk

  on blood and blondes, and though your husband looks like the Duke
of Cambridge, that's not what you love so much, ya dumb cluck,

  but his Henry James-Groucho Marx-Cajun shtick. Knock,
knock. Who's there? It's Moe, Larry, and Curly, nyuk nyuk nyuk.

Ava, darling, skin white as mayonnaise, eyes of cat-scratch topaz,
      zirconia smile, making *Mogambo* with Gable in Africa,
Bwana Clark, to you, baby, Grace Kelly tumbling the substitute daddy,
      you rolling in Swamp Sinatra. What did you see in him—dumb
crooner from Hoboken, a shrimp, and you in a gal's biggest fix,
      x- and y-chromosomes splitting in your deepest beauty, that toxic
ditch of burping and feeding on the horizon. You think you know
      what the years ahead hold—you left with the baby, Sinatra a cad.
Enemies or lovers—who's to say? Does anyone really change? Henry V,
      Vlad the Impaler, Saint Teresa of Avila—some do, but some
feel sucking the blood from a maiden's neck is all they can manage. You
      understood how beauty could take you only so far. Of course, if
God were in his heaven, we all might be film goddesses rather than fat
      timecard-punching factory workers with lacquered beehives, sewing
halter tops for girls whose primary job will always be painting their nails.
      Such a world begs you to believe in the Hindu idea of *maya*, which
is to say everything is illusion, kind of like the movies or theater or
      remember the time you found your boyfriend with your best friend? I
jump at the idea of *maya*, because though I try to be a good girl, right on cue
      quick as a bunny, the devil pulls me into his Buick, and the DJ
keeps playing "Who Do You Love"? Ava, you started out as a bit player: carhop,
      pretty hatcheck girl, ringsider, and then your gorgeous face was stuck
like candy on magazines and marquees from Sacramento to Buffalo,
      Orlando to Natchez. When you lay dying in London, did you feel
more alive than ever or was it like the story of Vishnu and the holy man
      Narada, who asks the god for the secret of *maya*? Vishnu says to him,
"Narada, dive into that lake," which he does and emerges a princess, slim,
      married to a powerful king. Her life is golden. She has many children,
owns palaces, her children have children, but her father and husband quarrel,
      lash out at each other until all her family are dead on the battlefield. No

person has known such grief. Her dear ones lie on the funeral pyre as daybreak

kindles its fire in the east, and she lights the flame, dives in, and comes up
queen no more, but Narada. "This," says Vishnu, "is *maya's* raj,

jailer extraordinaire. For whom do you weep, Narada?" This is the "Q"
really in "Q & A." For whom do we weep? In dreams we are Richard III,

ink-stained pen pushers, scullery maids, a hunched-over Laurence Olivier
starring as the evil king on stage, Marilyn Monroe on Harry Cohn's couch.

Here's to the movie queens with their nose jobs, snow jobs, blow jobs.
"The beauty thing was fun," Ava said later in Madrid walking along,

gabbing with a friend, passing Pam-Pam's, a local burger joint
under the white sky. "But I'd work at Pam-Pam's before I'd take off

for Hollywood and star in another crappy movie." O Vishnu,
Vishnu, make me dive into that lake every minute of my misbegotten life,

every time I forget I am Narada following the black *V*
wild birds make in an autumn sky. Here's to the mosquito, Lord,

drinking our blood, be we factory worker, star, wife, widow,
X-rated movie actress, saint, burger flipper, barfly, sporadic mechanic,

clown, or crone. Empty me of everything I am—sphinx, minx,
yogi, yeti, yenta, yodeling nun. Forgive me for being so dense, so numb.

Break my back with the beauty of the world. Throw me in solitary,
zip me into a shroud. Throw a match on the pyre, rend the veil of *maya*,

annex me as the Nazis annexed Poland, help me pass your pop quiz.

from 9 Sonnets from the Psalms

Hear my prayer, O Lord, though all I do all day is watch
old black-and-white movies on TV. Speak to me
through William Powell or Myrna Loy, solve the mystery
of my sloth. Show me the way to take a walk or catch
a cold, anything but read another exposé
of the Kennedys. Teach me to sing or at least play
the piano. For ten years I took lessons, and all
I learned was to hate Bach. Shake me up or down. Call
me names. Break my ears with AC/DC—I deserve far
worse. Rebuke me in front of my ersatz friends. Who cares?
They don't like me much anyway. Make me fat in lieu
of thin. Give me a break or don't. I'm a hundred million
molecules in search of an author. If that's you, thank you
for my skin. Without it I'd be in worse shape than I'm in.

I beseech thee, O Yellow Pages, help me find a number
for Barbara Stanwyck, because I need a tough broad
in my corner right now. She'll pour me a tumbler
of scotch or gin and tell me to buck up, show me the rod
she has hidden in her lingerie drawer. She has a temper,
yeah, but her laugh could take the wax off a cherry red
Chevy. "Shoot him," she'll say merrily, then scamper
off to screw an insurance company out of another wad
of dough. I'll be left holding the phone or worse, patsy
in another scheme, arrested by Edward G. Robinson
and sent to Sing Sing, while Barb lives like Gatsby
in Thailand or Tahiti, gambling the night away until the sun
rises in the east, because there are some things a girl can be sure
of, like morning coming after night's inconsolable lure.

Some days I feel like Janet Leigh in *Touch of Evil*—
I wake up, sunny and blond, but by the time midnight
rolls around I've been hijacked by Akim Tamiroff's
greasy thugs, shot up with heroin, framed for murder,
and I'm out cold in a border town jail. I didn't kill
Akim, of course, it was Hank Quinlan—drunk, overweight
Orson Welles—who for thirty-odd years as sheriff
has been framing creeps for crimes they maybe did. Enter
Mike Vargas, tall handsome Mexican cop—Charlton
Heston with a weird little mustache and a dark tan
from a can. "You don't talk like a Mexican," Welles
says, which speaks to me, because I can see how talking
like a Mexican could solve any number of roadside hells
I am currently running away from—well, walking.

The fool hath said in his heart, There is no God. I am
that Trinculo, wandering this blue-green island, drunk
in the company of clowns, waiting for a telegram
that will boost me out of my present jam. Oh, yes ma'am,
I'm in quicksand and thinking about *The Mummy* sunk
under a 4,000-year curse, or is it Caliban
skulking in the underbrush of my mind? What's this funk
that's grabbed me like a gorilla in love? If I can
shake-and-bake it into the next century, slam dunk
it into a FedEx box, send it to Kalamazoo,
then maybe I'll be able to breathe, but that low-down skunk,
my heart, won't quit beating for Prospero and his stew
of thunder and magic, so I stay up nights and scour
the sky for Zeus, his bolts shaking the midnight hour.

Ode to Airheads, Hairdos, Trains to and from Paris

For an hour on the train from Beauvais to Paris
      Nord I'm entertained by the conversation of three
American girls about their appointment the next
      day with a hairdresser, and if there is a subtext
to this talk, I'm missing it, though little else. Will bangs
      make them look too dykey? And layers, sometimes they hang
like the fur of a shaggy dog. Streaks, what about blond
      streaks? "Whore," they scream, laughing like a coven of wild
parrots, and after they have exhausted the present
      tense, they go on to the remembrance of hairdos past—
high school proms, botched perms, late-night drunken cuts. The Loch Ness
      Monster would be lost in their brains as in a vast, starless
sea, but they're happy, will marry, overpopulate
      the earth, which you can't say about many poets,
I think a few weeks later taking the 84
      bus to the hairdresser, where I'll spend three long hours
and leave with one of the best cuts of my life from Guy,
      who has a scar on his right cheek and is Israeli,
but before that I pass a hotel with a plaque—
      Attila József, great Hungarian poet, black
moods and penniless, lived there ten years before he threw
      himself under a train in Budapest. If we knew
what the years held, would we alter our choices, take the train
      at three-twenty instead of noon, walk in the rain
instead of taking the Métro? The time-travel films
      I adore speak to this very question: overwhelmed
by disease and war, the future sends Bruce Willis back
      to stop a madman. I could be waiting by the track
as József arrives in Paris, not with love but money,
      which seemed to be the missing ingredient, the honey

he needed to sweeten his tea. Most days I take the B
        line of the RER, and one of the stops is Drancy,
the way station for Jews rounded up by the Nazis
        before being sent in trains to the camps, but we can't see
those black-and-white figures in the Technicolor
        present like ghosts reminding us with their pallor
how dearly our circus of reds and golds has been purchased
        and how in an instant all those colors could be erased.

Mambo Cadillac

Drive me to the edge in your Mambo Cadillac,
       turn left at the graveyard and gas that baby, the black
night ringing with its holy roller scream. I'll clock
       you on the highway at three a.m., brother, amen, smack
the road as hard as we can, because I'm gonna crack
       the world in two, make a hoodoo soup with chicken necks,
a gumbo with a plutonium roux, a little snack
       before the dirt-and-jalapeño stew that will shuck
the skin right off your slinky hips, Mr. I'm-not-stuck
       in-a-middle-class-prison-with-someone-I-hate sack
of blues. Put on your high-wire shoes, Mr. Right, and stick
       with me. I'm going nowhere fast, the burlesque
queen of this dim scene, I want to feel the wind, the Glock
       in my mouth, going south, down-by-the-riverside shock
of the view. Take me to Shingles Fried Chicken Shack
       in your Mambo Cadillac. I was gone, but I'm back
for good this time. I've taken a shine to daylight. Crank
       up that radio, baby, put on some dance music
and shake your moneymaker, honey, rev it up to Mach
       two. I'm talking to you, Mr. Magoo. Sit up, check
out that blonde with the leopard print tattoo. O she'll lick
       the sugar right off your doughnut and bill you, too, speak
French while she do the do. *Parlez-vous français?* So, pick
       me up tonight at ten in your Mambo Cadillac
cause we got a date with the devil, so fill the tank
       with high-octane rhythm and blues, sugarcane, and shark
bait, too. We got some miles to cover, me and you, think
       Chile, Argentina, Peru. Take some time off work;
we're gonna be gone a lot longer than a week
       or two. Is this D-day or Waterloo? White or black—

it's up to you. We'll be in Mexico tonight. Pack

a razor, pack some glue. Things fall apart off the track,

and that's where we'll be, baby, in your Mambo Cadillac,

cause you're looking for love, but I'm looking for a wreck.

from Lingo Sonnets

Betty Boop's Bebop

Because I'm a cartoon airhead, people think it's a picnic
down on these mean streets. Sure, my skirt's short, but it's a crime,
fellows, how you give a frail the slip, leave her simmering,
hot and bothered. I have feelings, cardboard, but bordering on ennui,
just this side of *tristesse*. I may not be human, but I can kick
like one and bite and pinch, too. Don't forget, mister, I'm
not just a bimbo with a helium voice. I'm no rococo
parvenu pillhead. I've read your Rilke, your Montesquieu.
Really, I'm not as dumb as I look. Or maybe I am. Less
tries to be more, but ends up being nothing. My last beau
vetoed the philosophy of religion class in favor of pre-law,
exactly why I don't know, but I'm getting a glimmer. Stay
zany, the cartoonists tell me, and next year you'll play Cinderella.

Ganymede's Dream of Rosalind

Girlfriend, I am the boyfriend you never had—honeysuckle mouth,
indigent eyes, no rough Barbary beard when kissing me. Popinjay,
keep me in your little chest, nestle me in your cosy love hotel,
my mouthful of tangy violets, my pumpkin raviolo, my spoon
of crushed moonlight in June. On your breast let me sup,
quaff the nectar of your sweet quim, trim repository of dear
succulence. Only touch my cheek with your hand, and let
us again meet as we did that first time in Act II, Scene IV
when we ran away to the Forest of Arden. Rough sphinx,
you know my heart, because it's yours, too, and quartz,
altogether transparent stone. I yearn for you as a crab
craves the wet sand, a wildebeest the vast savannah, a toad
every mudhole and mossy shelf. Forget Orlando. I'll marry myself.

Karen, David, and I Stop across the Street from the Pitti Palace

In questi pressi fra il 1868 e il 1869 Fedor Mihailovic Dostoevskij compì
il romanzo L'Idiota

Knocking around after dinner at Alla Vecchia Bettola in the cool
Mediterranean evening, we are joined by Prince Myshkin,
of all people, because a plaque above a little paper shop
(quoted in the epigraph of this poem) tells us he was created here, or
so it says. Writers are such liars, and I should know. Fact:
until this moment I'd forgotten about the prince. It's like the TV
Western you watched with such rapture as a kid while eating a bowl of Trix;
you see a raccoon and suddenly remember the Lone Ranger's mask. Jeez,
and I loved Tonto. *Hi-yo, Silver,* I'm such a stale piece of crumb
cake, because during the dark night of 1974, Myshkin held my hand,
even though I was more like a shipwreck than a woman—mute, deaf,
gnawing on my own heart as if it were meat, your words a match
I lit to find this place—forever in your debt, Fedor Mihailovic Dostoevskij.

Nietzsche Explains the Übermensch to Lois Lane

No, no, no, no—he doesn't even have nerves of steel. No
point asking him to save you, ma'am, he's more likely to rescue
rain from the street. Born on your block, not Krypton, he's
terror with a capital *T*, the beautiful mind you
vain dames can't see for the mascara on your lashes. You saw
exactly nothing when you clapped eyes on him, a nerdy
zip, not even head of the class, just skulking in the back, a
brilliant light in a room full of blind men. But when he rises, havoc
descends on the world, lightning storms blister the earth, for he

fears nothing, feels nothing, sees everything. From the beginning
he's been a juggernaut, crushing everything in his path, from the Hindi
Jagannath, Lord of the World, a guise of the god Vishnu. A dark
Lex Luthor was more what I was thinking of than Superman, ma'am.

Zeus, It's Your Leda, Sweetie Pie

Zip up your toga, thunder thighs, that's Hera
barking like Cerberus on amphetamines. I was a skeptic,
don't you know, but you've got the equipment, as the
frigging king of the gods should. All the mortal gals are agog,
hinting for an invite to our next divine date, as if I
jump in your Caddy and we race toward a three-star snack,
lightning bolts setting the highway ablaze miles ahead. I'm
nervous about your wife. She blinded Tiresias, and Apollo
plays possum when she's around. Zeus, that's your cue—
reassure me. Don't think I want to move to Mt. Olympus.
Those relics are a snooze. Athena, there's dust on her tutu,
Venus's, too, so get a move on, or my Helen will wow
exactly no one and his horse. Let's dillydally, Ding-Dong Daddy.

Ode on Dictionaries

A-bomb is how it begins with a big bang on page
        one, a calculator of sorts whose centrifuge
begets *bedouin, bamboozle, breakdance,* and *berserk,*
        one of my mother's favorite words, hard knock
clerk of clichés that she is, at the moment *going ape*
        the current rave in the fundamentalist landscape
disguised as her brain, a rococo lexicon
        of Deuteronomy, Job, gossip, spritz, and neocon
ephemera all wrapped up in a pop burrito
        of movie star shenanigans, like a stray Cheeto
found in your pocket the day after you finish the bag,
        tastier than any oyster and champagne fueled *fugue*
gastronomique you have been pursuing in France
        for the past four months. This 82-year-old's rants
have taken their place with the dictionary I bought
        in the fourth grade, with so many gorgeous words I thought
I'd never plumb its depths. Right the first time, little girl,
        yet here I am still at it, trolling for pearls,
Japanese words vying with Bantu in a goulash
        I eat daily, sometimes gagging, sometimes with relish,
kleptomaniac in the candy store of language,
        slipping words in my pockets like a non-smudge
lipstick that smears with the first kiss. I'm the demented
        lady with sixteen cats. Sure, the house stinks, but those damned
mice have skeedaddled, though I kind of miss them, their cute
        little faces, the whiskers, those adorable gray suits.
No, all beasts are welcome in my menagerie, ark
        of inconsolable barks and meows, sharp-toothed shark,
OED of the deep ocean, sweet compendium
        of candy bars—Butterfingers, Mounds, and M&Ms—

packed next to the tripe and gizzards, trim and tackle

       of butchers and bakers, the painter's brush and spackle,

quarks and black holes of physicists' theory. I'm building

       my own book as a mason makes a wall or a gelding

runs round the track—brick by brick, step by step, word by word,

       jonquil by *gerrymander, syllabub* by *greensward,*

swordplay by *snapdragon,* a never-ending parade

       with clowns and funambulists in my own mouth, homemade

treasure chest of tongue and teeth, the brain's roustabout, rough

       unfurler of tents and trapezes, off-the-cuff

unruly troublemaker in the high church museum

       of the world. O mouth—boondoggle, auditorium,

viper, gulag, gumbo pot on a steamy August

       afternoon—what have you not given me? How I must

wear on you, my Samuel Johnson in a frock coat,

       lexicographer of silly thoughts, billy goat,

X-rated pornographic smut factory, scarfer

       of snacks, prissy smirker, late-night barfly,

you are the megaphone by which I bewitch the world

       or don't as the case may be. O chittering squirrel,

ziplock sandwich bag, sound off, shut up, gather your words

       into bouquets, folios, flocks of black and flaming birds.

Ode on My 45s, Insomnia, and My Poststructuralist Superego

O that life could be a day-and-night dance party
        with ginger ale, gin and tonics, or Bacardi
and Coke—who cares?—as long as the music keeps coming
        like a railroad train without brakes, the engine storming
down the tracks, the conductor's hair flying in the night
        air, like a tornado now, because I might
just take off, Little Richard screaming "Tutti Frutti"
        on my little portable record player, duty
fleeing like an *a-wop-bop-a-loo-bop* bomb on speed,
        and though my drug days are behind me, tonight I need
a fix of funk, because, lights low, "Little Red Corvette"
        will cure any ailment, even the knock-down Tourette's
that attacks at three a.m., super-ego Babette,
        snappy little twat with a French accent, legs, you bet,
in fishnet hose and a skirt up to here, snarling, "Slut,"
        though for emphasis she adds, *putain, salope*. "But, but,
but," I stutter, "I haven't slept with anyone but Dave
        for 25 years." "That's what you think, you bourgeois slave,"
and God knows I can let a detail slip, but you'd think
        I'd remember that, so excuse me while I sink
into a slough of despond so deep I can hear Chinese
        beneath my feet, but hold on—What's that?—It's "Please,
Mr. Postman," and the Marvelettes swing down and grab
        me up, for my rock-and-roll ids, Barbie and Babs,
have pushed back the rug, are doing the twist, drinking Tabs.
        "Forget that French bitch and her zombie hoard. You can stab
us in the back and call us Keith Richards," the girls coo,
        and then scream the lyrics of "I Put a Spell on You,"
because they've read Heidegger and Simone de Beauvoir,
        too, but it's not going stop them swinging *ce soir,*

dancing in the streets with Martha and the Vandellas

and drinking mai tais with little purple umbrellas,
for they reside in the land of a thousand dances,

where Wilson Pickett reigns supreme, while I freelance
at the funk bazaar, because sometimes Prince's "Kiss"

is all that stands between me and the darkening abyss,
and my girls are swinging their ponytails with Nadine,

Layla, Gloria, because we heard it through the grapevine
that not much longer will we be here, so let's go, girls,

down to the basement and say hello to the devil,
because his dress is red and trouble is on his mind,

and he's out searching for girls, but what does he find
when he gets to the party, revved up, ready to scare

our pants off—our pants are off and we're not fighting fair,
and who is the devil anyway but some ugly

guy with a goatee and fire coming from his ears. We
say, to hell with you, your minions, too, for there's music

in the air, and the night is shorter than your prick,
Satan, so move along, because we have some dancing

to do, in the streets, under the sheets. I'm not mincing
words here, because I've got three girls in one body. Wait,

that smells like religion, which I can do, especially the hate.

Ode on the Letter *M*

Midway through the alphabet, you are the tailored seam
        that ties *Adam* to *zephyr, atom* to *uranium,*
sword that takes up a new God, little lamb, turns him
        into a flame spewing Visigoth, and Byzantium
becomes Constantinople, the new Jerusalem,
        hallelujah, bombs away. Or are you the flim-flam
man working small towns in Mississippi—Troy, Denham,
        Tishomingo, Yazoo City—hawking a serum
that will cure everything—warts, impetigo, ringworm—
        fade wrinkles, spark a wilting libido. Oh, yes, ma'am,
dose your husband, and that rooster will crow again, thrum
        like a well-tuned violin. A masterful scam
it was until the day that pretty little schoolmarm
        purred like a pussy cat, locked you in her maximum
security prison with gold rings—aluminum
        siding your new game, the highway nothing but a dream
of freedom, because one letter can change grin to grim,
        plug to plum, slut to slum, a few blankets and wampum
can get you Manhattan, itself once New Amsterdam,
        because sometimes we seem to be a quorum
of idiots on a plague ship in a sea of phlegm
        and fog, rumors of disease flying like crows in the scum
of clouds heavy with hurricanes. Or the bride and groom
        in black and white, God bless their little Vietnam,
here's hoping for years of pound cake and hymns. There's a charm
        in myopia, witness Monet's chrysanthemum,
a blob of pink and blue, his lilies smears of thick cream
        on green. I take off my glasses when I can, though I'm
as lost as anyone, searching for the perfect dim sum
        restaurant, locked in my high gothic scriptorium,

scratching for words as rats scratch for cheese—Muenster, Edam,
> Livarot—for there are worlds in worlds—Mozart's requiem
the dark river Figaro sails on or *The Tin Drum*
> spawned by the SS. Who can guess the mysteries that cram
our brains? Not I, said the little black cat. Fee-fi-fo-fum,
> I smell the blood of everyone. Like Robert Mitchum
in *Cape Fear*, the ghouls are out, ripping the flesh off prom
> queens and popcorn girls, and as the storm clouds swarm
like killer bees, I'll be searching for my Tiny Tim,
> *om mani padme om,* God bless us, every worm.

ACKNOWLEDGMENTS

I would like to express my most ardent gratitude to the Guggenheim Foundation for the time to put this book together and write these new poems. I would also like to thank the Florida State College of Arts and Sciences for support during my Guggenheim year and the editors of the following magazines for publishing these poems:

New Poems: *Agni*: "17 Dollars" and "Ode to Wasting Time and Drawing Donatello's *David*"; *American Poetry Review*: "Ode to Forgetting the Year" and "Ode to Knots, Noise, Waking Up at Three, and Falling Asleep Reading to My Id"; *Five Points*: "On the Street of Divine Love" and "I'm Making Walt Whitman Soup"; *Ploughshares*: "Ode to the *Messiah*, Thai Horror Movies, and Everything I Don't Believe" and "Ode to the Triple"; *Plume*: "How to Pray"; *Poem-A-Day* (published online by the Academy of American Poets): "Ode to Lil' Kim"; *Southern Review*: "Ode to Red and Speedy" and "Reading Can Kill You"; *Spillway*: "Questions for My Body"; *Subtropics*: "Ode to Augurs, Ogres, Acorns, and Two or Three Things That Have Been Eating at My Heart Like a Wolverine in a Time of Famine"; *Yale Review*: "Ode to Skimpy Clothes and August in the Deep South."

Delirium (University of North Texas Press, 1995): *Another Chicago Magazine*: "The Language of Bees"; *Iowa Review*: "St. Anthony of the Floating Larynx" and "Toska"; *Ledge*: "Ova" and "Betrothal in B Minor"; *Paris Review*: "Delirium" and "Nose"; *Western Humanities Review*: "St. Clare's Underwear."

The Alphabet of Desire (New York University Press, 1999): *Five Points*: "Ode to the Lost Luggage Warehouse at the Rome Airport"; *Kenyon Review*: "Thinking of Galileo"; *Paris Review*: "Ode to Untoward Dreams"; *Parnassus*: "Achtung, My Princess, Goodnight"; *Southern Review*: "The Dream of the Red Drink," and "So Long, Roy"; *Southern Poetry Review*: "The Word"; *Western Humanities Review*: "Ode on My Wasted Youth."

Babel (University of Pittsburgh Press, 2004): *Boulevard*: "Ode to American English"; *Five Points*: "Ode to Barbecue"; *Indiana Review*: "Thus Spake the Mockingbird"; *Meridian*: "Ode on Satan's Power"; *Ploughshares*: "My Translation" and "Idolatry"; *Runes*: "O Deceitful Tongue"; *Southern Review*: "Ode to Hardware Stores" and "Ode to My 1977 Toyota."

All-Night Lingo Tango (University of Pittsburgh Press, 2009): *Five Points*: "Ode on My 45s, Insomnia, and My Poststructuralist Superego" and "Some Days I Feel Like Janet Leigh"; *Indiana Review*: "Ode to Airheads, Hairdos, Trains to and from Paris"; *Nightsun*: "The Fool Hath Said in His Heart," "Hear My Prayer," and "I Beseech Thee, O Yellow Pages"; *Pool*: "Mambo Cadillac"; *Salmagundi*: "Working at Pam-Pam's"; *Subtropics*: "Ode on Dictionaries"; *TriQuarterly*: "Betty Boop's Bebop," "Karen, David, and I Stop in Front of the Pitti Palace," "Ode to Anglo Saxon, Film Noir, and the Hundred Thousand Anxieties That Plague Me Like Demons in a Medieval Christian Allegory," "Ode on the Letter *M*," and "Zeus, It's Your Leda, Sweetie Pie"; *Verse*: "Ganymede Dreams of Rosaline," and "Nietzsche Explains the Übermench to Lois Lane."

And thanks to the following editors for reprinting the following poems:

"Ode to the Lost Luggage Warehouse at the Rome Airport" in *Best American Poetry 2000*, edited by Rita Dove and David Lehman, Scribners, 2001; "Delirium" in *The Paris Review Book of Heartbreak, Madness, Sex, Love, Betrayal, Outsiders, Intoxication, War, Whimsy, Horrors, God, Death, Dinner, Baseball, Travels, The Art of Writing, and Everything Else in the World Since 1953*, Picador, 2003; "Ode to American English" and "Ode on My 1977 Toyota" in *Good Poems for Hard Times*, edited by Garrison Keillor, Viking, 2005; "Ode to Airheads, Hairdos, Trains to and from Paris" in *Best American Poetry 2009*, edited by David Wagoner and David Lehman, Scribners, 2010; "Ganymede Dreams of Rosaline," "Nietzsche Explains the Übermench to Lois Lane" in *Best American Poetry 2010*, edited by Amy Gerstler and David Lehman, Scribners, 2011; "Mambo Cadillac" and "Ode to Hardware Stores" were in *Good Poems American Places*, edited by Garrison Keillor, Viking, 2011; "Thinking of Galileo" and "Hatred" in *The Penguin Anthology of Twentieth-Century American Poetry*, edited by Rita Dove, Penguin, 2011; Garrison Keillor read "Ode to American English" (October 14, 2006) and "Mambo Cadillac" (May 7, 2011) on his radio show *Prairie Home Companion*—I try not to hold it against him that his readings got a lot more laughs than mine do.

I hope Rimbaud lovers will forgive my very free translation at the beginning of this book.

As always I must thank my husband, David Kirby, for the blissful life he has set up for us and for always being smart and ready for fun, and especially for having the travel bug, too. I love being on the road with you, darling, whether it's our street or Outer Mongolia.

Stuart Riordan and I have collaborated for more than twenty years. She took the photograph for the cover of my first book, and her painting graces the cover of this book. I am so grateful for our ongoing conversation about the artistic process.

Florida State University's Study Abroad Program has been our travel agent as many of these poems will attest. Thank you to Mark Pietralunga and Karen Myers for many sublime summers in Italy. Also, thanks to Cynie Cory for helping me order the new poems in this book. And Albert Goldbarth, Tony Hoagland, Barbara Ras and Susan Wood for being friends indeed.

Magazine editors have been my reality check all through my writing life. When they are excited, then I know I am on to something, and when they send a poem back over and over I begin to have doubts about it. I thank you all, but especially Richard Howard, David Bottoms, Megan Sexton, Michael Griffith, Susan Hahn, Michael Keller, Herb Leibowitz, and Andrew Zawacki.

I also would like to thank Ed Ochester and the staff at the University of Pittsburgh Press. I am so grateful that my work has found such a home.

This book is dedicated to my sister, who is a brilliant artist, indefatigable party girl, and has the biggest heart in the world. Little did I know that the girl I shared a room with for so long would turn out to be my dearest friend.